Excitit
You (,
Now
That You're

18

ISBN 978-1547253807

Get a job. Go to college. Move out. Get a job. Go to college. Move out. Get a job. Go to college. Move out. Get a job. Go to college. Move out. Get a job. Go to college. Move out. Get a job. Go to college. Move out. Get a job. Move out. Get a job. Go to college. Move out. Get a job. Go to college. Move out. Get a job. Go to college. Move out. Get a job. Go to college. Move out. Get a job. Go to college. Move out. Get a job. Go to college. Move out. Get a job. Move out. Get a job. Go to college. Move out. Get a job. Go to college. Move out. Get a job. Go to college. Move out. Get a job. Go to college. Move out. Get a job. Go to college. Move out. Get a job. Go to college. Move out. Get a job. Move out. Get a job. Go to college. Move out. Get a job. Go to college. Move out. Get a job. Go to college. Move out. Get a job. Go to college. Move out. Get a job. Go to college. Move out. Get a job. Go to college. Move out. Get a job.

 Move out. Get a job. Go to college. Move out. Get a job. Go to college. Move out. Get a job. Go to college. Move out. Get a job. Go to college. Move out. Get a job. Go to college. Move out. Get a job. Go to college. Move out. Get a job. Move out. Get a job. Go to college. Move out. Get a job. Go to college. Move out. Get a job. Go to college. Move out. Get a job. Go to college. Move out. Get a job. Go to college. Move out. Get a job. Go to college. Move out. Get a job. Go to college. Move out. Get a job. Go to college. Move out. Get a job. Go to college. Move out. Get a job. Go to college. Move out. Get a job. Go to college. Move out. Get a job. Move out. Get a job. Go to college. Move out. Get a job. Go to college. Move out. Get a job. Go to college. Move

out. Get a job. Go to college. Move out. Get a job. Go to college. Move out. Get a job. Move out. Get a job. Go to college.   Move out. Get a job. Go to college. Move out. Get a job. Go to college. Move out. Get a job. Go to college.   Move out. Get a job. Go to college. Move out. Get a job. Go to college. Move out. Get a job.

Move out. Get a job. Go to college.   Move out. Get a job. Go to college. Move out. Get a job. Go to college. Move out. Get a job. Go to college.   Move out. Get a job. Go to college. Move out. Get a job. Go to college. Move out. Get a job.

Move out. Get a job. Go to college.   Move out. Get a job. Go to college. Move out. Get a job. Go to college. Move out. Get a job. Go to college.   Move out. Get a job. Go to college. Move out. Get a job. Go to college. Move out. Get a job.

Move out. Get a job. Go to college.   Move out. Get a job. Go to college. Move out. Get a job. Go to college.   Move out. Get a job. Go to college. Move out. Get a job. Go to college. Move out. Get a job. Move out. Get a job. Go to college.   Move out. Get a job. Go to college. Move out. Get a job. Go to college.   Move out. Get a job. Go to college. Move out. Get a job. Go to college. Move out. Get a job.

Move out. Get a job. Go to college.   Move out. Get a job. Go to college. Move out. Get a job. Go to college. Move out. Get a job. Go to college.   Move out. Get a job. Go to college. Move out. Get a job. Go to college. Move out. Get a job. Move out. Get a job. Go to college.   Move out. Get a job. Go to college. Move out. Get a job. Go to college.   Move out. Get a job. Go to college. Move out. Get a job. Go to college. Move out. Get a job.

Move out. Get a job. Go to college.   Move out. Get a job. Go to college. Move out. Get a job. Go to college.

Move out. Get a job. Go to college. Move out. Get a job. Go to college. Move out. Get a job. Go to college. Move out. Get a job.

Move out. Get a job. Go to college. Move out. Get a job. Go to college. Move out. Get a job. Go to college. Move out. Get a job. Go to college. Move out. Get a job. Go to college. Move out. Get a job.

Move out. Get a job. Go to college. Move out. Get a job. Go to college. Move out. Get a job. Go to college. Move out. Get a job. Go to college. Move out. Get a job. Go to college. Move out. Get a job.

Move out. Get a job. Go to college. Move out. Get a job. Go to college. Move out. Get a job. Go to college. Move out. Get a job. Go to college. Move out. Get a job. Go to college. Move out. Get a job. Go to college. Move out. Get a job. Go to college. Move out. Get a job. Go to college. Move out. Get a job. Go to college. Move out. Get a job. Move out. Get a job. Go to college. Move out. Get a job. Go to college. Move out. Get a job. Go to college. Move out. Get a job. Go to college. Move out. Get a job. Go to college. Move out. Get a job. Go to college. Move out. Get a job. Move out. Get a job. Go to college. Move out. Get a job. Go to college. Move out. Get a job. Go to college. Move out. Get a job. Go to college. Move out. Get a job. Move out. Get a job. Go to college. Move out. Get a job. Go to college. Move out. Get a job. Go to college. Move out. Get a job. Go to college. Move out. Get a job. Go to college. Move out.

Get a job. Go to college. Move out. Get a job. Go to college. Move out. Get a job. Go to college. Move out. Get a job. Move out. Get a job. Go to college. Move out. Get a job. Go to college. Move out. Get a job. Go to college. Move out. Get a job. Go to college. Move out. Get a job. Go to college. Move out. Get a job. Go to college. Move out. Get a job. Move out. Get a job. Go to college. Move out. Get a job. Go to college. Move out. Get a job. Go to college. Move out. Get a job. Go to college. Move out. Get a job. Move out. Get a job. Move out. Get a job. Go to college. Move out. Get a job. Go to college. Move out. Get a job. Go to college. Move out. Get a job. Go to college. Move out. Get a job. Go to college. Move out. Get a job. Go to college. Move out. Get a job. Go to college. Move out. Get a job. Move out. Get a job. Go to college. Move out. Get a job. Go to college. Move out. Get a job. Go to college. Move out. Get a job. Go to college. Move out. Get a job. Go to college. Move out. Get a job. Go to college. Move out. Get a job. Move out. Get a job. Go to college. Move out. Get a job. Go to college. Move out. Get a job. Go to college. Move out. Get a job. Go to college. Move out. Get a job. Go to college. Move out. Get a job. Go to college. Move out. Get a job. Move out. Get a job. Go to college. Move out. Get a job. Go to college. Move out. Get a job. Go to college. Move out. Get a job. Go to college. Move out. Get a job. Go to college. Move out. Get a job. Move out. Get a job. Go to college. Move out. Get a job. Go to college. Move out. Get a job. Go to college. Move out. Get a job. Go to college. Move out. Get a job. Go to college. Move out. Get a job. Go to college. Move out. Get a job. Move out. Get a job. Go to college. Move out. Get a job. Go

to college. Move out. Get a job. Go to college. Move out.
Get a job. Go to college.   Move out. Get a job. Go to
college. Move out. Get a job. Go to college. Move out.
Get a job. Move out. Get a job. Go to college.   Move
out. Get a job. Go to college. Move out. Get a job. Go
to college. Move out. Get a job. Go to college.   Move
out. Get a job. Go to college. Move out. Get a job. Go
to college. Move out. Get a job. Move out. Get a job. Go
to college.   Move out. Get a job. Go to college. Move
out. Get a job. Go to college. Move out. Get a job. Go
to college.   Move out. Get a job. Go to college. Move
out. Get a job. Go to college. Move out. Get a job. Move
out. Get a job. Go to college.   Move out. Get a job. Go
to college. Move out. Get a job. Go to college. Move out.
Get a job. Go to college.   Move out. Get a job. Go to
college. Move out. Get a job. Go to college. Move out.
Get a job. Move out. Get a job. Go to college.   Move
out. Get a job. Go to college. Move out. Get a job. Go
to college. Move out. Get a job. Go to college.   Move
out. Get a job. Go to college. Move out. Get a job. Go
to college. Move out. Get a job. Move out. Get a job. Go
to college.   Move out. Get a job. Go to college. Move
out. Get a job. Go to college. Move out. Get a job. Go
to college.   Move out. Get a job. Go to college. Move
out. Get a job. Go to college. Move out. Get a job.

Move out. Get a job. Go to college.   Move out. Get a
job. Go to college. Move out. Get a job. Go to college.
Move out. Get a job. Go to college.   Move out. Get a
job. Go to college. Move out. Get a job. Go to college.
 Move out. Get a job. Move out. Get a job. Go to
college. Move out. Get a job. Go to college. Move out.
Get a job. Go to college. Move out. Get a job. Go to
college. Move out. Get a job. Go to college. Move out.
Get a job. Go to college. Move out. Get a job. Move out.
Get a job. Go to college.   Move out. Get a job. Go to
college. Move out. Get a job. Go to college. Move out.
Get a job. Go to college.   Move out. Get a job. Go to
college. Move out. Get a job. Go to college. Move out.

Get a job. Move out. Get a job. Go to college. Move out. Get a job. Go to college. Move out. Get a job. Go to college. Move out. Get a job. Go to college. Move out. Get a job. Go to college. Move out. Get a job. Go to college. Move out. Get a job. Move out. Get a job. Go to college. Move out. Get a job. Go to college. Move out. Get a job. Go to college. Move out. Get a job. Go to college. Move out. Get a job. Go to college. Move out. Get a job.

Move out. Get a job. Go to college. Move out. Get a job. Go to college. Move out. Get a job. Go to college. Move out. Get a job. Go to college. Move out. Get a job. Go to college. Move out. Get a job. Go to college. Move out. Get a job.

Move out. Get a job. Go to college. Move out. Get a job. Go to college. Move out. Get a job. Go to college. Move out. Get a job. Go to college. Move out. Get a job. Go to college. Move out. Get a job. Go to college. Move out. Get a job.

Move out. Get a job. Go to college. Move out. Get a job. Go to college. Move out. Get a job. Go to college. Move out. Get a job. Go to college. Move out. Get a job. Go to college. Move out. Get a job. Go to college. Move out. Get a job. Move out. Get a job. Go to college. Move out. Get a job. Go to college. Move out. Get a job. Go to college. Move out. Get a job. Go to college. Move out. Get a job. Go to college. Move out. Get a job.

Move out. Get a job. Go to college. Move out. Get a job. Go to college. Move out. Get a job. Go to college. Move out. Get a job. Go to college. Move out. Get a job. Go to college. Move out. Get a job. Go to college. Move out. Get a job. Move out. Get a job. Go to college. Move out. Get a job. Go to college. Move out. Get a job. Go to college. Move out. Get a job. Go to college. Move out. Get a job. Go to college. Move out. Get a job.

8

Move out. Get a job. Go to college. Move out. Get a job. Go to college. Move out. Get a job. Go to college. Move out. Get a job. Go to college. Move out. Get a job. Go to college. Move out. Get a job. Go to college. Move out. Get a job.

Move out. Get a job. Go to college. Move out. Get a job. Go to college. Move out. Get a job. Go to college. Move out. Get a job. Go to college. Move out. Get a job. Go to college. Move out. Get a job. Go to college. Move out. Get a job.

Move out. Get a job. Go to college. Move out. Get a job. Go to college. Move out. Get a job. Go to college. Move out. Get a job. Go to college. Move out. Get a job. Go to college. Move out. Get a job. Go to college. Move out. Get a job.

Move out. Get a job. Go to college. Move out. Get a job. Go to college. Move out. Get a job. Go to college. Move out. Get a job. Go to college. Move out. Get a job. Go to college. Move out. Get a job. Go to college. Move out. Get a job. Move out. Get a job. Go to college. Move out. Get a job. Go to college. Move out. Get a job. Go to college. Move out. Get a job. Go to college. Move out. Get a job. Go to college. Move out. Get a job. Move out. Get a job. Go to college. Move out. Get a job. Go to college. Move out. Get a job. Go to college. Move out. Get a job. Go to college. Move out. Get a job. Go to college. Move out. Get a job. Move out. Get a job. Go to college. Move out. Get a job. Go to college. Move out. Get a job. Go to college. Move out. Get a job. Go to college. Move out. Get a job. Go to college. Move out. Get a job. Go to college. Move out. Get a job. Go to college. Move out. Get a job. Go to college. Move out. Get a job. Go to college. Move out. Get a job. Go to college. Move out. Get a job. Go to college. Move out. Get a job. Move out. Get a job. Go to college. Move out. Get a job. Go to college. Move out. Get a job. Go to college. Move out. Get a job. Go to college. Move out. Get a job. Go to college. Move out. Get a job. Go to college. Move out. Get a job. Move out. Get a job. Go to college. Move out. Get a job. Go to college. Move out. Get a job. Go to college. Move out. Get a job. Go to college. Move out. Get a job. Go to college. Move out. Get a job. Go to college. Move out. Get a job. Move out. Get a job. Go to college. Move out. Get a job. Go to college. Move out. Get a job. Go to college. Move out. Get a job. Go to college. Move out. Get a job. Go to college. Move out. Get a job. Go to college. Move out. Get a job. Move out. Get a job. Go to college. Move out. Get a job. Go to college. Move out. Get a job. Go to college. Move out. Get a job. Go to college. Move out. Get a job. Go to college. Move out. Get a job. Go to college. Move out. Get a job. Move out. Get a job. Go to college. Move out. Get a job. Go to college. Move out. Get a job. Go to college. Move out. Get a job. Go to college. Move out. Get a job. Go to college. Move out. Get a job. Go to college. Move out. Get a job. Move out. Get a job. Go to college. Move out. Get a job. Go to college. Move out. Get a job. Go to college. Move out. Get a job. Go to college. Move out. Get a job. Go to college. Move out. Get a job. Go to college. Move out. Get a job. Move out. Get a job. Go to college. Move out. Get a job. Go to college. Move out. Get a job. Go to college. Move out. Get a job. Go to college. Move out. Get a job. Go to college. Move out. Get a job. Go to college. Move out. Get a job. Move out. Get a job. Go to college. Move out. Get a job. Go to college. Move out. Get a job. Go to college. Move out. Get a job. Go to college. Move out. Get a job. Go to college. Move out. Get a job. Go to college. Move out. Get a job. Move out. Get a job. Go to college. Move out. Get a job. Go to college. Move out. Get a job. Go to college. Move out. Get a job. Go to college. Move

out. Get a job. Go to college. Move out. Get a job. Move
out. Get a job. Go to college.   Move out. Get a job. Go
to college. Move out. Get a job. Go to college. Move out.
Get a job. Go to college.   Move out. Get a job. Go to
college. Move out. Get a job. Go to college. Move out.
Get a job. Move out. Get a job. Go to college.   Move
out. Get a job. Go to college. Move out. Get a job. Go
to college. Move out. Get a job. Go to college.   Move
out. Get a job. Go to college. Move out. Get a job. Go
to college. Move out. Get a job.

Move out. Get a job. Go to college.   Move out. Get a
job. Go to college. Move out. Get a job. Go to college.
Move out. Get a job. Go to college.   Move out. Get a
job. Go to college. Move out. Get a job. Go to college.
Move out. Get a job. Move out. Get a job. Go to
college.   Move out. Get a job. Go to college. Move out.
Get a job. Go to college. Move out. Get a job. Go to
college.   Move out. Get a job. Go to college. Move out.
Get a job. Go to college. Move out. Get a job. Move out.
Get a job. Go to college.   Move out. Get a job. Go to
college. Move out. Get a job. Go to college. Move out.
Get a job. Go to college.   Move out. Get a job. Go to
college. Move out. Get a job. Go to college. Move out.
Get a job. Move out. Get a job. Go to college.   Move
out. Get a job. Go to college. Move out. Get a job. Go
to college. Move out. Get a job. Go to college.   Move
out. Get a job. Go to college. Move out. Get a job. Go
to college. Move out. Get a job.

Move out. Get a job. Go to college.   Move out. Get a
job. Go to college. Move out. Get a job. Go to college.
Move out. Get a job. Go to college.   Move out. Get a
job. Go to college. Move out. Get a job. Go to college.
Move out. Get a job. Move out. Get a job. Go to
college.   Move out. Get a job. Go to college. Move out.
Get a job. Go to college. Move out. Get a job. Go to
college.   Move out. Get a job. Go to college. Move out.
Get a job. Go to college. Move out. Get a job. Move out.
Get a job. Go to college.   Move out. Get a job. Go to

college. Move out. Get a job. Go to college. Move out. Get a job. Go to college.   Move out. Get a job. Go to college. Move out. Get a job. Go to college. Move out. Get a job. Move out. Get a job. Go to college.   Move out. Get a job. Go to college. Move out. Get a job. Go to college. Move out. Get a job. Go to college.   Move out. Get a job. Go to college. Move out. Get a job. Go to college. Move out. Get a job. Move out. Get a job. Go to college.   Move out. Get a job. Go to college. Move out. Get a job. Go to college.   Move out. Get a job. Go to college. Move out. Get a job.

Move out. Get a job. Go to college.   Move out. Get a job. Go to college. Move out. Get a job. Go to college. Move out. Get a job. Go to college.   Move out. Get a job. Go to college. Move out. Get a job. Go to college. Move out. Get a job.

Move out. Get a job. Go to college.   Move out. Get a job. Go to college. Move out. Get a job. Go to college. Move out. Get a job. Go to college.   Move out. Get a job. Go to college. Move out. Get a job. Go to college. Move out. Get a job.

Move out. Get a job. Go to college.   Move out. Get a job. Go to college. Move out. Get a job. Go to college. Move out. Get a job. Go to college.   Move out. Get a job. Go to college. Move out. Get a job. Go to college. Move out. Get a job. Move out. Get a job. Go to college.   Move out. Get a job. Go to college. Move out. Get a job. Go to college. Move out.   Move out. Get a job. Go to college. Move out. Get a job. Go to college. Move out. Get a job.

Move out. Get a job. Go to college.   Move out. Get a job. Go to college. Move out. Get a job. Go to college. Move out. Get a job. Go to college.   Move out. Get a job. Go to college. Move out. Get a job. Go to college. Move out. Get a job. Move out. Get a job. Go to college.   Move out. Get a job. Go to college. Move out.

Get a job. Go to college. Move out. Get a job. Go to college.   Move out. Get a job. Go to college. Move out. Get a job. Go to college. Move out. Get a job.

Move out. Get a job. Go to college.   Move out. Get a job. Go to college. Move out. Get a job. Go to college. Move out. Get a job. Go to college.   Move out. Get a job. Go to college. Move out. Get a job. Go to college. Move out. Get a job.

Move out. Get a job. Go to college.   Move out. Get a job. Go to college. Move out. Get a job. Go to college. Move out. Get a job. Go to college.   Move out. Get a job. Go to college. Move out. Get a job. Go to college. Move out. Get a job.

Move out. Get a job. Go to college.   Move out. Get a job. Go to college. Move out. Get a job. Go to college. Move out. Get a job. Go to college.   Move out. Get a job. Go to college. Move out. Get a job. Go to college. Move out. Get a job.

Move out. Get a job. Go to college.   Move out. Get a job. Go to college. Move out. Get a job. Go to college. Move out. Get a job. Go to college.   Move out. Get a job. Go to college. Move out. Get a job. Go to college. Move out. Get a job. Move out. Get a job. Go to college.   Move out. Get a job. Go to college. Move out. Get a job. Go to college.   Move out. Get a job. Go to college. Move out. Get a job. Go to college. Move out. Get a job. Move out. Get a job. Go to college.   Move out. Get a job. Go to college. Move out. Get a job. Go to college.   Move out. Get a job. Go to college. Move out. Get a job. Go to college. Move out. Get a job. Move out. Get a job. Go to college.   Move out. Get a job. Go to college. Move out. Get a job. Go to college.   Move out. Get a job. Go to college. Move out. Get a job. Go to college. Move out. Get a job. Go to college. Move out. Get a job. Go to college.   Move out. Get a job. Go to college. Move out. Get a job. Go to college. Move out. Get a job. Go to college. Move out. Get a job. Go to college. Move out. Get a job. Move out. Get a job. Go to college. Move out. Get a job. Go to college. Move out. Get a job. Go to college. Move out. Get a job. Go to college. Move out. Get a job. Go to college. Move out. Get a job. Go to college. Move out. Get a job. Go to college. Move out. Get a job. Move out. Get a job. Go to college. Move out. Get a job. Go to college. Move out. Get a job. Go to college. Move out. Get a job. Go to college. Move out. Get a job. Go to college. Move out. Get a job. Move out. Get a job. Go to college. Move out. Get a job. Go to college. Move out. Get a job. Go to college. Move out. Get a job. Go to college. Move out. Get a job. Go to college. Move out. Get a job. Go to college. Move out. Get a job. Go to college. Move out. Get a job. Move out. Get a job. Go to college. Move out. Get a job. Go to college. Move out. Get a job. Go to college. Move out. Get a job. Go to college. Move out. Get a job. Go to college. Move out. Get a job. Go to college. Move out. Get a job. Go to college. Move out. Get a job. Go to college. Move out. Get a job. Go to college. Move out. Get a job. Go to college. Move out. Get a job. Move out. Get a job. Go to college. Move out. Get a job. Go to college. Move out. Get a job. Go to college. Move out. Get a job. Go to college. Move out. Get a job. Go to college. Move out. Get a job. Go

to college. Move out. Get a job. Go to college. Move
out. Get a job. Go to college. Move out. Get a job. Go
to college. Move out. Get a job. Go to college. Move
out. Get a job. Go to college. Move out. Get a job. Move
out. Get a job. Go to college. Move out. Get a job. Go
to college. Move out. Get a job. Go to college. Move out.
Get a job. Go to college. Move out. Get a job. Go to
college. Move out. Get a job. Go to college. Move out.
Get a job. Move out. Get a job. Go to college. Move
out. Get a job. Go to college. Move out. Get a job. Go
to college. Move out. Get a job. Go to college. Move
out. Get a job. Go to college. Move out. Get a job. Go
to college. Move out. Get a job.

Move out. Get a job. Go to college. Move out. Get a
job. Go to college. Move out. Get a job. Go to college.
Move out. Get a job. Go to college. Move out. Get a
job. Go to college. Move out. Get a job. Go to college.
Move out. Get a job. Move out. Get a job. Go to
college. Move out. Get a job. Go to college. Move out.
Get a job. Go to college. Move out. Get a job. Go to
college. Move out. Get a job. Go to college. Move out.
Get a job. Go to college. Move out. Get a job. Move out.
Get a job. Go to college. Move out. Get a job. Go to
college. Move out. Get a job. Go to college. Move out.
Get a job. Go to college. Move out. Get a job. Go to
college. Move out. Get a job. Go to college. Move out.
Get a job. Move out. Get a job. Go to college. Move
out. Get a job. Go to college. Move out. Get a job. Go
to college. Move out. Get a job. Go to college. Move
out. Get a job. Go to college. Move out. Get a job. Go
to college. Move out. Get a job.

Move out. Get a job. Go to college. Move out. Get a
job. Go to college. Move out. Get a job. Go to college.
Move out. Get a job. Go to college. Move out. Get a
job. Go to college. Move out. Get a job. Go to college.
Move out. Get a job. Move out. Get a job. Go to
college. Move out. Get a job. Go to college. Move out.
Get a job. Go to college. Move out. Get a job. Go to

college. Move out. Get a job. Go to college. Move out. Get a job. Go to college. Move out. Get a job. Move out. Get a job. Go to college. Move out. Get a job. Go to college. Move out. Get a job. Go to college. Move out. Get a job. Go to college. Move out. Get a job. Go to college. Move out. Get a job. Go to college. Move out. Get a job. Move out. Get a job. Go to college. Move out. Get a job. Go to college. Move out. Get a job. Go to college. Move out. Get a job. Go to college. Move out. Get a job. Go to college. Move out. Get a job. Go to college. Move out. Get a job. Move out. Get a job. Go to college. Move out. Get a job. Go to college. Move out. Get a job. Go to college. Move out. Get a job. Go to college. Move out. Get a job. Go to college. Move out. Get a job.

Move out. Get a job. Go to college. Move out. Get a job. Go to college. Move out. Get a job. Go to college. Move out. Get a job. Go to college. Move out. Get a job. Go to college. Move out. Get a job.

Move out. Get a job. Go to college. Move out. Get a job. Go to college. Move out. Get a job. Go to college. Move out. Get a job. Go to college. Move out. Get a job. Go to college. Move out. Get a job. Go to college. Move out. Get a job.

Move out. Get a job. Go to college. Move out. Get a job. Go to college. Move out. Get a job. Go to college. Move out. Get a job. Go to college. Move out. Get a job. Go to college. Move out. Get a job. Go to college. Move out. Get a job. Go to college. Move out. Get a job. Go to college. Move out. Get a job. Go to college. Move out. Get a job.

Move out. Get a job. Go to college. Move out. Get a job. Go to college. Move out. Get a job. Go to college. Move out. Get a job. Go to college. Move out. Get a job. Go to college. Move out. Get a job. Go to college. Move out. Get a job. Move out. Get a job. Go to college. Move out. Get a job. Go to college. Move out. Get a job. Go to college. Move out. Get a job. Go to college. Move out. Get a job. Go to college. Move out. Get a job. Go to college. Move out.

Move out. Get a job. Go to college. Move out. Get a job. Go to college. Move out. Get a job. Go to college. Move out. Get a job. Go to college. Move out. Get a job. Go to college. Move out. Get a job.

Move out. Get a job. Go to college. Move out. Get a job. Go to college. Move out. Get a job. Go to college. Move out. Get a job. Go to college. Move out. Get a job. Go to college. Move out. Get a job.

Move out. Get a job. Go to college. Move out. Get a job. Go to college. Move out. Get a job. Go to college. Move out. Get a job. Go to college. Move out. Get a job. Go to college. Move out. Get a job.

Move out. Get a job. Go to college. Move out. Get a job. Go to college. Move out. Get a job. Go to college. Move out. Get a job. Go to college. Move out. Get a job. Move out. Get a job. Go to college. Move out. Get a job. Go to college. Move out. Get a job. Go to college. Move out. Get a job. Go to college. Move out. Get a job. Move out. Get a job. Go to college. Move out. Get a job. Go to college. Move out. Get a job. Go to college. Move out. Get a job. Go to college. Move out. Get a job. Move out. Get a job. Go to college. Move out. Get a job. Go to college. Move out. Get a job. Go to college. Move out. Get a job. Go to college. Move out. Get a job. Go to college. Move out. Get a job. Move out. Get a job. Go to college. Move out. Get a job. Go to college. Move out. Get a job. Go to college. Move out. Get a job. Go to college. Move out. Get a job. Go to college. Move out. Get a job. Go to college. Move out. Get a job. Move out. Get a job. Go to college. Move out. Get a job. Go to college. Move out. Get a job. Go to college. Move out. Get a job. Go to college. Move out. Get a job. Go to college. Move out. Get a job. Go to college. Move out. Get a job. Move out. Get a job. Go to college. Move out. Get a job. Go to college. Move out. Get a job. Go to college. Move out. Get a job. Go to college. Move out. Get a job. Go to college. Move out. Get a job. Go to college. Move out. Get a job. Move out. Get a job. Go to college. Move out. Get a job. Go to college. Move out. Get a job. Go to college. Move out. Get a job. Move out. Get a job. Go to college. Move out. Get a job. Go to college. Move out. Get a job. Go to college. Move out. Get a job. Go to college. Move out. Get a job. Go to college. Move out. Get a job. Go to college. Move out. Get a job. Go to college. Move out. Get a job. Move out. Get a job. Go to college. Move out. Get a job. Go to college. Move out. Get a job. Go to college. Move out. Get a job. Go to college. Move out. Get a job. Move out. Get a job. Go to college. Move out. Get a job. Go to college. Move out. Get a job. Go

to college. Move out. Get a job. Go to college.   Move
out. Get a job. Go to college. Move out. Get a job. Go
to college. Move out. Get a job. Move out. Get a job. Go
to college.   Move out. Get a job. Go to college. Move
out. Get a job. Go to college. Move out. Get a job. Go
to college.   Move out. Get a job. Go to college. Move
out. Get a job. Go to college. Move out. Get a job. Move
out. Get a job. Go to college.   Move out. Get a job. Go
to college. Move out. Get a job. Go to college. Move out.
Get a job. Go to college.   Move out. Get a job. Go to
college. Move out. Get a job. Go to college. Move out.
Get a job. Move out. Get a job. Go to college.   Move
out. Get a job. Go to college. Move out. Get a job. Go
to college. Move out. Get a job. Go to college.   Move
out. Get a job. Go to college. Move out. Get a job. Go
to college. Move out. Get a job.

Move out. Get a job. Go to college.   Move out. Get a
job. Go to college. Move out. Get a job. Go to college.
Move out. Get a job. Go to college.   Move out. Get a
job. Go to college. Move out. Get a job. Go to college.
Move out. Get a job. Move out. Get a job. Go to
college.   Move out. Get a job. Go to college. Move out.
Get a job. Go to college. Move out. Get a job. Go to
college.   Move out. Get a job. Go to college. Move out.
Get a job. Go to college. Move out. Get a job. Move out.
Get a job. Go to college.   Move out. Get a job. Go to
college. Move out. Get a job. Go to college. Move out.
Get a job. Go to college.   Move out. Get a job. Go to
college. Move out. Get a job. Go to college. Move out.
Get a job. Move out. Get a job. Go to college.   Move
out. Get a job. Go to college. Move out. Get a job. Go
to college. Move out. Get a job. Go to college.   Move
out. Get a job. Go to college. Move out. Get a job. Go
to college. Move out. Get a job.

Move out. Get a job. Go to college.   Move out. Get a
job. Go to college. Move out. Get a job. Go to college.
Move out. Get a job. Go to college.   Move out. Get a
job. Go to college. Move out. Get a job. Go to college.

Move out. Get a job. Move out. Get a job. Go to college. Move out. Get a job. Go to college. Move out. Get a job. Go to college. Move out. Get a job. Go to college. Move out. Get a job. Go to college. Move out. Get a job. Go to college. Move out. Get a job. Move out. Get a job. Go to college. Move out. Get a job. Go to college. Move out. Get a job. Go to college. Move out. Get a job. Go to college. Move out. Get a job. Go to college. Move out. Get a job. Move out. Get a job. Go to college. Move out. Get a job. Go to college. Move out. Get a job. Go to college. Move out. Get a job. Go to college. Move out. Get a job. Go to college. Move out. Get a job. Go to college. Move out. Get a job. Go to college. Move out. Get a job. Go to college. Move out. Get a job. Go to college. Move out. Get a job. Go to college. Move out. Get a job.

Move out. Get a job. Go to college. Move out. Get a job. Go to college. Move out. Get a job. Go to college. Move out. Get a job. Go to college. Move out. Get a job. Go to college. Move out. Get a job. Go to college. Move out. Get a job.

Move out. Get a job. Go to college. Move out. Get a job. Go to college. Move out. Get a job. Go to college. Move out. Get a job. Go to college. Move out. Get a job. Go to college. Move out. Get a job. Go to college. Move out. Get a job.

Move out. Get a job. Go to college. Move out. Get a job. Go to college. Move out. Get a job. Go to college. Move out. Get a job. Go to college. Move out. Get a job. Move out. Get a job. Go to college. Move out. Get a job. Go to college. Move out. Get a job. Go to college. Move out. Get a job. Go to college. Move out. Get a job. Go to college. Move out. Get a job.

Move out. Get a job. Go to college. Move out. Get a job. Go to college. Move out. Get a job. Go to college. Move out. Get a job. Go to college. Move out. Get a job. Go to college. Move out. Get a job. Go to college. Move out. Get a job. Move out. Get a job. Go to college. Move out. Get a job. Go to college. Move out. Get a job. Go to college. Move out. Get a job. Go to college. Move out. Get a job. Go to college. Move out. Get a job.

Move out. Get a job. Go to college. Move out. Get a job. Go to college. Move out. Get a job. Go to college. Move out. Get a job. Go to college. Move out. Get a job. Go to college. Move out. Get a job.

Move out. Get a job. Go to college. Move out. Get a job. Go to college. Move out. Get a job. Go to college. Move out. Get a job. Go to college. Move out. Get a job. Go to college. Move out. Get a job.

Move out. Get a job. Go to college. Move out. Get a job. Go to college. Move out. Get a job. Go to college. Move out. Get a job. Go to college. Move out. Get a job. Go to college. Move out. Get a job.

Move out. Get a job. Go to college. Move out. Get a job. Go to college. Move out. Get a job. Go to college. Move out. Get a job. Go to college. Move out. Get a job. Go to college. Move out. Get a job. Move out. Get a job. Go to college. Move out. Get a job. Go to college. Move out. Get a job. Go to college. Move out. Get a job. Go to college. Move out. Get a job. Go to college. Move out. Get a job. Move out. Get a job. Go to college. Move out. Get a job. Go to college. Move out. Get a job. Go to college. Move out. Get a job. Go to college. Move out.

Get a job. Move out. Get a job. Go to college. Move out. Get a job. Go to college. Move out. Get a job. Go to college. Move out. Get a job. Go to college. Move out. Get a job. Go to college. Move out. Get a job. Go to college. Move out. Get a job. Move out. Get a job. Go to college. Move out. Get a job. Go to college. Move out. Get a job. Go to college. Move out. Get a job. Go to college. Move out. Get a job. Go to college. Move out. Get a job. Move out. Get a job. Go to college. Move out. Get a job. Go to college. Move out. Get a job. Go to college. Move out. Get a job. Go to college. Move out. Get a job. Go to college. Move out. Get a job. Go to college. Move out. Get a job. Go to college. Move out. Get a job. Go to college. Move out. Get a job. Go to college. Move out. Get a job. Go to college. Move out. Get a job. Move out. Get a job. Go to college. Move out. Get a job. Go to college. Move out. Get a job. Go to college. Move out. Get a job. Go to college. Move out. Get a job. Go to college. Move out. Get a job. Go to college. Move out. Get a job. Go to college. Move out. Get a job. Go to college. Move out. Get a job. Go to college. Move out. Get a job. Move out. Get a job. Go to college. Move out. Get a job. Go to college. Move out. Get a job. Go to college. Move out. Get a job. Go to college. Move out. Get a job. Go to college. Move out. Get a job. Go to college. Move out. Get a job. Move out. Get a job. Go to college. Move out. Get a job. Go to college. Move out. Get a job. Go to college. Move out. Get a job. Go to college. Move out. Get a job. Go to college. Move out. Get a job. Go to college. Move out. Get a job. Go to college. Move out. Get a job. Go to college. Move out. Get a job. Go to college. Move out. Get a job. Move out. Get a job. Go to college. Move out. Get a job. Go to college. Move out. Get a job. Go to college. Move out. Get a job. Go to college. Move out. Get a job. Go to college. Move out. Get a job. Go to college. Move out. Get a job. Move out. Get a job. Go to college. Move out. Get a job. Go to college. Move out. Get a job. Go to college. Move out. Get a job. Go to college. Move out. Get a job. Go to college. Move out. Get a job. Move out. Get a job. Go to college. Move out. Get a job. Go to college. Move out. Get a job. Go to college. Move out. Get a job. Go to college. Move out. Get a job. Go to college. Move out. Get a job. Move out. Get a job. Go to college. Move out. Get a job. Go to college. Move out. Get a job. Go to college. Move out. Get a job. Go to college. Move out. Get a job. Go to college. Move out. Get a job.

Move out. Get a job. Go to college. Move out. Get a job. Go to college. Move out. Get a job. Go to college. Move out. Get a job. Go to college. Move out. Get a job. Go to college. Move out. Get a job. Go to college. Move out. Get a job. Move out. Get a job. Go to college. Move out. Get a job. Go to college. Move out. Get a job. Go to college. Move out. Get a job. Go to college. Move out. Get a job. Go to college. Move out. Get a job. Move out. Get a job. Go to college. Move out. Get a job. Go to college. Move out. Get a job. Go to college. Move out. Get a job. Go to college. Move out. Get a job. Go to college. Move out. Get a job. Move out. Get a job. Go to college. Move out. Get a job. Go to college. Move out. Get a job. Go to college. Move out. Get a job. Go to college. Move out. Get a job. Go to college. Move out. Get a job.

Move out. Get a job. Go to college.   Move out. Get a job. Go to college. Move out. Get a job. Go to college. Move out. Get a job. Go to college.   Move out. Get a job. Go to college. Move out. Get a job. Go to college. Move out. Get a job. Move out. Get a job. Go to college. Move out. Get a job. Go to college. Move out. Get a job. Go to college. Move out. Get a job. Go to college. Move out. Get a job. Go to college. Move out. Get a job. Go to college. Move out. Get a job. Move out. Get a job.   Move out. Get a job. Go to college. Move out. Get a job. Go to college. Move out. Get a job. Go to college.   Move out. Get a job. Go to college. Move out. Get a job. Go to college. Move out. Get a job. Move out. Get a job. Go to college.   Move out. Get a job. Go to college. Move out. Get a job. Go to college.   Move out. Get a job. Go to college. Move out. Get a job. Move out. Get a job. Go to college.   Move out. Get a job. Go to college. Move out. Get a job. Go to college.   Move out. Get a job. Go to college. Move out. Get a job. Go to college. Move out. Get a job. Go to college. Move out. Get a job.

Move out. Get a job. Go to college.   Move out. Get a job. Go to college. Move out. Get a job. Go to college. Move out. Get a job. Go to college.   Move out. Get a job. Go to college. Move out. Get a job. Go to college. Move out. Get a job.

Move out. Get a job. Go to college.   Move out. Get a job. Go to college. Move out. Get a job. Go to college. Move out. Get a job. Go to college.   Move out. Get a job. Go to college. Move out. Get a job. Go to college. Move out. Get a job.

Move out. Get a job. Go to college.   Move out. Get a job. Go to college. Move out. Get a job. Go to college. Move out. Get a job. Go to college.   Move out. Get a job. Go to college. Move out. Get a job. Go to college. Move out. Get a job. Move out. Get a job. Go to

college.   Move out. Get a job. Go to college. Move out. Get a job. Go to college. Move out. Get a job. Go to college.   Move out. Get a job. Go to college. Move out. Get a job. Go to college. Move out. Get a job.

Move out. Get a job. Go to college.   Move out. Get a job. Go to college. Move out. Get a job. Go to college. Move out. Get a job. Go to college.   Move out. Get a job. Go to college. Move out. Get a job. Go to college. Move out. Get a job. Move out. Get a job. Go to college.   Move out. Get a job. Go to college. Move out. Get a job. Go to college.   Move out. Get a job. Go to college. Move out. Get a job. Go to college. Move out. Get a job.

Move out. Get a job. Go to college.   Move out. Get a job. Go to college. Move out. Get a job. Go to college. Move out. Get a job. Go to college.   Move out. Get a job. Go to college. Move out. Get a job. Go to college. Move out. Get a job.

Move out. Get a job. Go to college.   Move out. Get a job. Go to college. Move out. Get a job. Go to college. Move out. Get a job. Go to college.   Move out. Get a job. Go to college. Move out. Get a job. Go to college. Move out. Get a job.

Move out. Get a job. Go to college.   Move out. Get a job. Go to college. Move out. Get a job. Go to college.   Move out. Get a job. Go to college. Move out. Get a job. Go to college. Move out. Get a job.

Move out. Get a job. Go to college.   Move out. Get a job. Go to college. Move out. Get a job. Go to college.   Move out. Get a job. Go to college. Move out. Get a job. Go to college. Move out. Get a job. Move out. Get a job. Go to college.   Move out. Get a job. Go to college. Move out. Get a job. Go to college.   Move out. Get a job. Go to college. Move out.

Get a job. Go to college. Move out. Get a job. Move out. Get a job. Go to college. Move out. Get a job. Go to college. Move out. Get a job. Go to college. Move out. Get a job. Go to college. Move out. Get a job. Go to college. Move out. Get a job. Go to college. Move out. Get a job. Move out. Get a job. Go to college. Move out. Get a job. Go to college. Move out. Get a job. Go to college. Move out. Get a job. Go to college. Move out. Get a job. Go to college. Move out. Get a job. Go to college. Move out. Get a job. Move out. Get a job. Go to college. Move out. Get a job. Go to college. Move out. Get a job. Go to college. Move out. Get a job. Go to college. Move out. Get a job. Move out. Get a job. Go to college. Move out. Get a job. Go to college. Move out. Get a job. Go to college. Move out. Get a job. Go to college. Move out. Get a job. Go to college. Move out. Get a job. Go to college. Move out. Get a job. Move out. Get a job. Go to college. Move out. Get a job. Go to college. Move out. Get a job. Go to college. Move out. Get a job. Go to college. Move out. Get a job. Go to college. Move out. Get a job. Go to college. Move out. Get a job. Move out. Get a job. Go to college. Move out. Get a job. Go to college. Move out. Get a job. Go to college. Move out. Get a job. Go to college. Move out. Get a job. Go to college. Move out. Get a job. Go to college. Move out. Get a job. Go to college.   Move out. Get a job. Go to college. Move out. Get a job. Go to college. Move out. Get a job. Move out. Get a job. Go to college.   Move out. Get a job. Go to college. Move out. Get a job. Go to college. Move out. Get a job. Go to college.   Move out. Get a job. Go to college. Move out. Get a job. Go to college. Move out. Get a job. Move out. Get a job. Go to college.   Move out. Get a job. Go to college. Move out. Get a job. Go to college.   Move out. Get a job. Go to college. Move out. Get a job. Go to college. Move out. Get a job. Move out. Get a job. Go to college.   Move out. Get a job. Go to college. Move out. Get a job. Go to college. Move out. Get a job. Go to college.   Move out. Get a job. Go to college. Move out. Get a job. Go to college. Move out. Get a job. Move out. Get a job. Go to college.   Move out. Get a job. Go to college. Move out. Get a job. Go to college.   Move out. Get a job. Go to college. Move out. Get a job. Go to college.   Move out. Get a job. Go to college. Move out. Get a job. Go to college. Move out. Get a job. Go to college.   Move out. Get a job. Go to college. Move out. Get a job. Move out. Get a job. Go to college.   Move out. Get a job. Go to college. Move out. Get a job. Go to college.   Move out. Get a job. Go to college. Move out. Get a job. Go to college. Move out. Get a job. Go to college.

Move out. Get a job. Go to college.   Move out. Get a job. Go to college. Move out. Get a job. Go to college. Move out. Get a job. Go to college.   Move out. Get a job. Go to college. Move out. Get a job. Go to college. Move out. Get a job. Move out. Get a job. Go to college.   Move out. Get a job. Go to college. Move out. Get a job. Go to college. Move out. Get a job. Go to college.   Move out. Get a job. Go to college. Move out. Get a job. Go to college. Move out. Get a job. Move out. Get a job. Go to college.   Move out. Get a job. Go to college. Move out. Get a job. Go to college. Move out. Get a job. Go to college.   Move out. Get a job. Go to college. Move out. Get a job. Go to college. Move out. Get a job. Move out. Get a job. Go to college.   Move

out. Get a job. Go to college. Move out. Get a job. Go to college. Move out. Get a job. Go to college. Move out. Get a job. Go to college. Move out. Get a job. Go to college. Move out. Get a job.

Move out. Get a job. Go to college. Move out. Get a job. Go to college. Move out. Get a job. Go to college. Move out. Get a job. Go to college. Move out. Get a job. Go to college. Move out. Get a job. Go to college. Move out. Get a job. Move out. Get a job. Go to college. Move out. Get a job. Go to college. Move out. Get a job. Go to college. Move out. Get a job. Go to college. Move out. Get a job. Go to college. Move out. Get a job. Move out. Get a job. Go to college. Move out. Get a job. Go to college. Move out. Get a job. Go to college. Move out. Get a job. Go to college. Move out. Get a job. Go to college. Move out. Get a job. Move out. Get a job. Go to college. Move out. Get a job. Go to college. Move out. Get a job. Go to college. Move out. Get a job. Go to college. Move out. Get a job. Go to college. Move out. Get a job. Go to college. Move out. Get a job. Go to college. Move out. Get a job. Go to college. Move out. Get a job. Go to college. Move out. Get a job.

Move out. Get a job. Go to college. Move out. Get a job. Go to college. Move out. Get a job. Go to college. Move out. Get a job. Go to college. Move out. Get a job. Go to college. Move out. Get a job. Go to college. Move out. Get a job.

Move out. Get a job. Go to college. Move out. Get a job. Go to college. Move out. Get a job. Go to college. Move out. Get a job. Go to college. Move out. Get a job. Go to college. Move out. Get a job. Go to college. Move out. Get a job.

Move out. Get a job. Go to college. Move out. Get a
job. Go to college. Move out. Get a job. Go to college.
Move out. Get a job. Go to college. Move out. Get a
job. Go to college. Move out. Get a job. Go to college.
Move out. Get a job. Move out. Get a job. Go to
college. Move out. Get a job. Go to college. Move out.
Get a job. Go to college. Move out. Get a job. Go to
college. Move out. Get a job. Go to college. Move out.
Get a job. Go to college. Move out. Get a job.

Move out. Get a job. Go to college. Move out. Get a
job. Go to college. Move out. Get a job. Go to college.
Move out. Get a job. Go to college. Move out. Get a
job. Go to college. Move out. Get a job. Go to college.
Move out. Get a job. Move out. Get a job. Go to
college. Move out. Get a job. Go to college. Move out.
Get a job. Go to college. Move out. Get a job. Go to
college. Move out. Get a job. Go to college. Move out.
Get a job. Go to college. Move out. Get a job.

Move out. Get a job. Go to college. Move out. Get a
job. Go to college. Move out. Get a job. Go to college.
Move out. Get a job. Go to college. Move out. Get a
job. Go to college. Move out. Get a job. Go to college.
Move out. Get a job.

Move out. Get a job. Go to college. Move out. Get a
job. Go to college. Move out. Get a job. Go to college.
Move out. Get a job. Go to college. Move out. Get a
job. Go to college. Move out. Get a job. Go to college.
Move out. Get a job.

Move out. Get a job. Go to college. Move out. Get a
job. Go to college. Move out. Get a job. Go to college.
Move out. Get a job. Go to college. Move out. Get a
job. Go to college. Move out. Get a job. Go to college.
Move out. Get a job.

Move out. Get a job. Go to college. Move out. Get a
job. Go to college. Move out. Get a job. Go to college.
Move out. Get a job. Go to college. Move out. Get a

job. Go to college. Move out. Get a job. Go to college. Move out. Get a job. Move out. Get a job. Go to college. Move out. Get a job. Go to college. Move out. Get a job. Go to college. Move out. Get a job. Go to college. Move out. Get a job. Go to college. Move out. Get a job. Go to college. Move out. Get a job. Move out. Get a job. Go to college. Move out. Get a job. Go to college. Move out. Get a job. Go to college. Move out. Get a job. Go to college. Move out. Get a job. Go to college. Move out. Get a job. Go to college. Move out. Get a job. Move out. Get a job. Go to college. Move out. Get a job. Go to college. Move out. Get a job. Go to college. Move out. Get a job. Go to college. Move out. Get a job. Go to college. Move out. Get a job. Move out. Get a job. Go to college. Move out. Get a job. Go to college. Move out. Get a job. Go to college. Move out. Get a job. Go to college. Move out. Get a job. Go to college. Move out. Get a job. Move out. Get a job. Go to college. Move out. Get a job. Go to college. Move out. Get a job. Go to college. Move out. Get a job. Go to college. Move out. Get a job. Go to college. Move out. Get a job. Move out. Get a job. Go to college. Move out. Get a job. Go to college. Move out. Get a job. Go to college. Move out. Get a job. Go to college. Move out. Get a job. Go to college. Move out. Get a job. Move out. Get a job. Go to college. Move out. Get a job. Go to college. Move out. Get a job. Go

to college. Move out. Get a job. Go to college.   Move
out. Get a job. Go to college. Move out. Get a job. Go
to college. Move out. Get a job. Move out. Get a job. Go
to college.   Move out. Get a job. Go to college. Move
out. Get a job. Go to college. Move out. Get a job. Go
to college.   Move out. Get a job. Go to college. Move
out. Get a job. Go to college. Move out. Get a job. Move
out. Get a job. Go to college.   Move out. Get a job. Go
to college. Move out. Get a job. Go to college. Move out.
Get a job. Go to college.   Move out. Get a job. Go to
college. Move out. Get a job. Go to college. Move out.
Get a job. Move out. Get a job. Go to college.   Move
out. Get a job. Go to college. Move out. Get a job. Go
to college. Move out. Get a job. Go to college.   Move
out. Get a job. Go to college. Move out. Get a job. Go
to college. Move out. Get a job. Move out. Get a job. Go
to college.   Move out. Get a job. Go to college. Move
out. Get a job. Go to college. Move out. Get a job. Go
to college.   Move out. Get a job. Go to college. Move
out. Get a job. Go to college. Move out. Get a job. Move
out. Get a job. Go to college.   Move out. Get a job. Go
to college. Move out. Get a job. Go to college. Move out.
Get a job. Go to college.   Move out. Get a job. Go to
college. Move out. Get a job. Go to college. Move out.
Get a job. Move out. Get a job. Go to college.   Move
out. Get a job. Go to college. Move out. Get a job. Go
to college. Move out. Get a job. Go to college.   Move
out. Get a job. Go to college. Move out. Get a job. Go
to college. Move out. Get a job.

Move out. Get a job. Go to college.   Move out. Get a
job. Go to college. Move out. Get a job. Go to college.
Move out. Get a job. Go to college.   Move out. Get a
job. Go to college. Move out. Get a job. Go to college.
Move out. Get a job. Move out. Get a job. Go to
college.   Move out. Get a job. Go to college. Move out.
Get a job. Go to college. Move out. Get a job. Go to
college.   Move out. Get a job. Go to college. Move out.
Get a job. Go to college. Move out. Get a job. Move out.

31

Get a job. Go to college. Move out. Get a job. Go to college. Move out. Get a job. Go to college. Move out. Get a job. Go to college. Move out. Get a job. Go to college. Move out. Get a job. Go to college. Move out. Get a job. Move out. Get a job. Go to college. Move out. Get a job. Go to college. Move out. Get a job. Go to college. Move out. Get a job. Go to college. Move out. Get a job. Go to college. Move out. Get a job.

Move out. Get a job. Go to college. Move out. Get a job. Go to college. Move out. Get a job. Go to college. Move out. Get a job. Go to college. Move out. Get a job. Go to college. Move out. Get a job. Move out. Get a job. Go to college. Move out. Get a job. Go to college. Move out. Get a job. Go to college. Move out. Get a job. Go to college. Move out. Get a job. Go to college. Move out. Get a job. Move out. Get a job. Go to college. Move out. Get a job. Go to college. Move out. Get a job. Go to college. Move out. Get a job. Go to college. Move out. Get a job. Go to college. Move out. Get a job. Go to college. Move out. Get a job. Move out. Get a job. Go to college. Move out. Get a job. Go to college. Move out. Get a job. Go to college. Move out. Get a job. Go to college. Move out. Get a job. Move out. Get a job. Go to college. Move out. Get a job. Go to college. Move out. Get a job. Go to college. Move out. Get a job. Go to college. Move out. Get a job. Go to college. Move out. Get a job.

Move out. Get a job. Go to college. Move out. Get a job. Go to college. Move out. Get a job. Go to college. Move out. Get a job. Go to college. Move out. Get a job. Go to college. Move out. Get a job. Go to college. Move out. Get a job.

Move out. Get a job. Go to college.   Move out. Get a job. Go to college. Move out. Get a job. Go to college. Move out. Get a job. Go to college.   Move out. Get a job. Go to college. Move out. Get a job. Go to college. Move out. Get a job.

Move out. Get a job. Go to college.   Move out. Get a job. Go to college. Move out. Get a job. Go to college. Move out. Get a job. Go to college.   Move out. Get a job. Go to college. Move out. Get a job. Go to college. Move out. Get a job. Move out. Get a job. Go to college.   Move out. Get a job. Go to college. Move out. Get a job. Go to college.   Move out. Get a job. Go to college. Move out. Get a job. Go to college. Move out. Get a job.

Move out. Get a job. Go to college.   Move out. Get a job. Go to college. Move out. Get a job. Go to college. Move out. Get a job. Go to college.   Move out. Get a job. Go to college. Move out. Get a job. Move out. Get a job. Go to college.   Move out. Get a job. Go to college. Move out. Get a job. Go to college.   Move out. Get a job. Go to college. Move out. Get a job. Go to college. Move out. Get a job.

Move out. Get a job. Go to college.   Move out. Get a job. Go to college. Move out. Get a job. Go to college. Move out. Get a job. Go to college.   Move out. Get a job. Go to college. Move out. Get a job. Go to college. Move out. Get a job.

Move out. Get a job. Go to college.   Move out. Get a job. Go to college. Move out. Get a job. Go to college. Move out. Get a job. Go to college.   Move out. Get a job. Go to college. Move out. Get a job. Go to college. Move out. Get a job.

Move out. Get a job. Go to college.   Move out. Get a job. Go to college. Move out. Get a job. Go to college.   Move out. Get a

job. Go to college. Move out. Get a job. Go to college. Move out. Get a job.

Move out. Get a job. Go to college.   Move out. Get a job. Go to college. Move out. Get a job. Go to college. Move out. Get a job. Go to college.   Move out. Get a job. Go to college. Move out. Get a job. Go to college. Move out. Get a job. Move out. Get a job. Go to college.   Move out. Get a job. Go to college. Move out. Get a job. Go to college. Move out. Get a job. Go to college.   Move out. Get a job. Go to college. Move out. Get a job. Go to college. Move out. Get a job. Go to college.   Move out. Get a job. Go to college. Move out. Get a job. Go to college. Move out. Get a job. Go to college.   Move out. Get a job. Go to college. Move out. Get a job. Go to college. Move out. Get a job. Move out. Get a job. Go to college.   Move out. Get a job. Go to college. Move out. Get a job. Go to college. Move out. Get a job. Go to college.   Move out. Get a job. Go to college. Move out. Get a job. Go to college. Move out. Get a job. Move out. Get a job. Go to college.   Move out. Get a job. Go to college. Move out. Get a job. Go to college.   Move out. Get a job. Go to college. Move out. Get a job. Go to college. Move out. Get a job. Go to college.   Move out. Get a job. Go to college. Move out. Get a job. Go to college. Move out. Get a job. Go to college.   Move out. Get a job. Go to college. Move out. Get a job. Go to college. Move out. Get a job. Move out. Get a job. Go to college.   Move out. Get a job. Go to college.   Move out. Get a job. Go to college. Move out. Get a job. Go to college. Move out. Get a job. Go to college.   Move out. Get a job. Go to college. Move out. Get a job. Go to college. Move out. Get a job. Go to college.   Move out. Get a job. Go to college. Move out. Get a job. Go to college. Move out. Get a job. Move out. Get a job. Go to college.   Move out. Get a job. Go to college. Move out. Get a job. Go to college. Move out. Get a job. Go to college. Move out. Get a job. Go to college. Move out. Get a job. Go to college. Move out. Get a job. Move out. Get a job. Go to college. Move out. Get a job. Go to college. Move out. Get a job. Go to college. Move out. Get a job. Go to college. Move out. Get a job. Go to college. Move out. Get a job. Go to college. Move out. Get a job. Move out. Get a job. Go to college. Move out. Get a job. Go to college. Move out. Get a job. Go to college. Move out. Get a job. Go to college. Move out. Get a job. Go to college. Move out. Get a job. Go to college. Move out. Get a job. Move out. Get a job. Go to college. Move out. Get a job. Go to college. Move out. Get a job. Go to college. Move out. Get a job. Go to college. Move out. Get a job. Go to college. Move out. Get a job. Go to college. Move out. Get a job. Move out. Get a job. Go to college. Move out. Get a job. Go to college. Move out. Get a job. Go to college. Move out. Get a job. Go to college. Move out. Get a job. Go to college. Move out. Get a job. Go to college. Move out. Get a job. Move out. Get a job. Go to college. Move out. Get a job. Go to college. Move out. Get a job. Go to college. Move out. Get a job. Go to college. Move out. Get a job. Go to college. Move out. Get a job. Go to college. Move out. Get a job. Move out. Get a job. Go to college. Move out. Get a job. Go to college. Move out. Get a job. Go to college. Move out. Get a job. Go to college. Move out. Get a job. Go to college. Move out. Get a job. Go to college. Move out. Get a job. Move out. Get a job. Go to college. Move out. Get a job. Go to college. Move out. Get a job. Go to college. Move out. Get a job. Go to college. Move out. Get a job. Go to college. Move out. Get a job. Go to college. Move out. Get a job.

Move out. Get a job. Go to college. Move out. Get a job. Go to college. Move out. Get a job. Go to college. Move out. Get a job. Go to college. Move out. Get a job. Go to college. Move out. Get a job. Go to college.

Move out. Get a job. Move out. Get a job. Go to college. Move out. Get a job. Go to college. Move out. Get a job. Go to college. Move out. Get a job. Go to college. Move out. Get a job. Go to college. Move out. Get a job. Go to college. Move out. Get a job. Move out. Get a job. Go to college. Move out. Get a job. Go to college. Move out. Get a job. Go to college. Move out. Get a job. Go to college. Move out. Get a job. Go to college. Move out. Get a job. Go to college. Move out. Get a job. Move out. Get a job. Go to college. Move out. Get a job. Go to college. Move out. Get a job. Go to college. Move out. Get a job. Go to college. Move out. Get a job. Go to college. Move out. Get a job.

Move out. Get a job. Go to college. Move out. Get a job. Go to college. Move out. Get a job. Go to college. Move out. Get a job. Go to college. Move out. Get a job. Go to college. Move out. Get a job. Move out. Get a job. Go to college. Move out. Get a job. Go to college. Move out. Get a job. Go to college. Move out. Get a job. Go to college. Move out. Get a job. Move out. Get a job. Go to college. Move out. Get a job. Go to college. Move out. Get a job. Go to college. Move out. Get a job. Go to college. Move out. Get a job. Go to college. Move out. Get a job. Move out. Get a job. Go to college. Move out. Get a job. Go to college. Move out. Get a job. Go to college. Move out. Get a job. Go to college. Move out. Get a job. Move out. Get a job. Go to college. Move out. Get a job. Go to college. Move out. Get a job. Go to college. Move out. Get a job. Go to college. Move out. Get a job. Go to college. Move out. Get a job.

Move out. Get a job. Go to college. Move out. Get a job. Go to college. Move out. Get a job. Go to college.

Move out. Get a job. Go to college.   Move out. Get a job. Go to college. Move out. Get a job. Go to college. Move out. Get a job.

Move out. Get a job. Go to college.   Move out. Get a job. Go to college. Move out. Get a job. Go to college. Move out. Get a job. Go to college.   Move out. Get a job. Go to college. Move out. Get a job. Go to college. Move out. Get a job.

Move out. Get a job. Go to college.   Move out. Get a job. Go to college. Move out. Get a job. Go to college. Move out. Get a job. Go to college.   Move out. Get a job. Go to college. Move out. Get a job. Go to college. Move out. Get a job. Move out. Get a job. Go to college.   Move out. Get a job. Go to college. Move out. Get a job. Go to college.   Move out. Get a job. Go to college. Move out. Get a job. Go to college. Move out. Get a job.

Move out. Get a job. Go to college.   Move out. Get a job. Go to college. Move out. Get a job. Go to college. Move out. Get a job. Go to college.   Move out. Get a job. Go to college. Move out. Get a job. Go to college. Move out. Get a job. Move out. Get a job. Go to college.   Move out. Get a job. Go to college. Move out. Get a job. Go to college.   Move out. Get a job. Go to college. Move out. Get a job. Go to college. Move out. Get a job.

Move out. Get a job. Go to college.   Move out. Get a job. Go to college. Move out. Get a job. Go to college.   Move out. Get a job. Go to college. Move out. Get a job. Go to college. Move out. Get a job.

Move out. Get a job. Go to college.   Move out. Get a job. Go to college. Move out. Get a job. Go to college.   Move out. Get a job. Go to college. Move out. Get a job. Go to college. Move out. Get a job.

Move out. Get a job. Go to college.   Move out. Get a job. Go to college. Move out. Get a job. Go to college. Move out. Get a job. Go to college.   Move out. Get a job. Go to college. Move out. Get a job. Go to college. Move out. Get a job.

Move out. Get a job. Go to college.   Move out. Get a job. Go to college. Move out. Get a job. Go to college. Move out. Get a job. Go to college.   Move out. Get a job. Go to college. Move out. Get a job. Go to college. Move out. Get a job. Move out. Get a job. Go to college.   Move out. Get a job. Go to college. Move out. Get a job. Go to college. Move out. Get a job. Go to college.   Move out. Get a job. Go to college. Move out. Get a job. Go to college. Move out. Get a job. Go to college.   Move out. Get a job. Go to college. Move out. Get a job. Go to college. Move out. Get a job. Go to college.   Move out. Get a job. Go to college. Move out. Get a job. Go to college. Move out. Get a job. Move out. Get a job. Go to college.   Move out. Get a job. Go to college. Move out. Get a job. Go to college.   Move out. Get a job. Go to college. Move out. Get a job. Go to college. Move out. Get a job. Go to college. Move out. Get a job. Move out. Get a job. Go to college.   Move out. Get a job. Go to college. Move out. Get a job. Go to college.   Move out. Get a job. Go to college. Move out. Get a job. Move out. Get a job. Go to college.   Move out. Get a job. Go to college. Move out. Get a job. Go to college. Move out. Get a job. Go to college.   Move out. Get a job. Go to college. Move out. Get a job. Go to college. Move out. Get a job. Go to college.   Move out. Get a job. Go to college. Move out. Get a job. Move out. Get a job. Go to college.   Move out. Get a job. Go to college. Move out. Get a job. Go to college.   Move out. Get a job. Go to college. Move out. Get a job. Go to college. Move out. Get a job. Go to college. Move out. Get a job. Go to college. Move out. Get a job. Move out. Get a job. Go to college. Move out. Get a job. Go to college. Move out. Get a job. Go to college. Move out. Get a job. Go to college. Move out. Get a job. Go to college. Move out. Get a job. Go to college. Move out. Get a job. Move out. Get a job. Go to college. Move out. Get a job. Go to college. Move out. Get a job. Go to college. Move out. Get a job. Go to college. Move out. Get a job. Go to college. Move out. Get a job. Go to college. Move out. Get a job. Move out. Get a job. Go to college. Move out. Get a job. Go to college. Move out. Get a job. Go to college. Move out. Get a job. Go to college. Move out. Get a job. Go to college. Move out. Get a job. Go to college. Move out. Get a job. Move out. Get a job. Go to college. Move out. Get a job. Go to college. Move out. Get a job. Go to college. Move out. Get a job. Go to college. Move out. Get a job. Go to college. Move out. Get a job. Go to college. Move out. Get a job. Move out. Get a job. Go to college. Move out. Get a job. Go to college. Move out. Get a job. Go to college. Move out. Get a job. Go to college. Move out. Get a job. Go to college. Move out. Get a job. Go to college. Move out. Get a job. Move out. Get a job. Go to college. Move out. Get a job. Go to college. Move out. Get a job. Go to college. Move out. Get a job. Go to college. Move out. Get a job. Go to college. Move out. Get a job. Go to college. Move out. Get a job.

Move out. Get a job. Go to college.   Move out. Get a job. Go to college. Move out. Get a job. Go to college. Move out. Get a job. Go to college.   Move out. Get a job. Go to college. Move out. Get a job. Go to college. Move out. Get a job. Move out. Get a job. Go to college.   Move out. Get a job. Go to college. Move out. Get a job. Go to college. Move out. Get a job. Go to college.   Move out. Get a job. Go to college. Move out. Get a job. Move out. Get a job. Go to college.   Move out. Get a job. Go to college. Move out. Get a job. Go to college. Move out. Get a job. Go to college.   Move out. Get a job. Go to college. Move out. Get a job. Move out. Get a job. Go to college.   Move out. Get a job. Go to college. Move out. Get a job. Go to college. Move out. Get a job. Go to college.   Move out. Get a job. Go to college. Move out. Get a job.

Move out. Get a job. Go to college.   Move out. Get a job. Go to college. Move out. Get a job. Go to college. Move out. Get a job. Go to college.   Move out. Get a job. Go to college. Move out. Get a job. Go to college. Move out. Get a job. Move out. Get a job. Go to college.   Move out. Get a job. Go to college. Move out. Get a job. Go to college. Move out. Get a job. Go to college.   Move out. Get a job. Go to college. Move out. Get a job. Move out. Get a job. Go to college.   Move out. Get a job. Go to college. Move out. Get a job. Go to college. Move out. Get a job. Go to college.   Move out. Get a job. Go to college. Move out. Get a job. Move out. Get a job. Go to college.   Move out. Get a job. Go to college. Move out. Get a job. Go to college.   Move out. Get a job. Go to college. Move out. Get a job. Go to college. Move out. Get a job. Move out. Get a job. Go to college.   Move out. Get a job. Go to college. Move out. Get a job. Go to college. Move out. Get a job. Go to college.   Move out. Get a job. Go to college. Move out. Get a job. Go to college. Move out. Get a job.

Move out. Get a job. Go to college.   Move out. Get a job. Go to college. Move out. Get a job. Go to college. Move out. Get a job. Go to college.   Move out. Get a job. Go to college. Move out. Get a job. Go to college. Move out. Get a job.

Move out. Get a job. Go to college.   Move out. Get a job. Go to college. Move out. Get a job. Go to college. Move out. Get a job. Go to college.   Move out. Get a job. Go to college. Move out. Get a job. Go to college. Move out. Get a job.

Move out. Get a job. Go to college.   Move out. Get a job. Go to college. Move out. Get a job. Go to college. Move out. Get a job. Go to college.   Move out. Get a job. Go to college. Move out. Get a job. Go to college. Move out. Get a job. Move out. Get a job. Go to college.   Move out. Get a job. Go to college. Move out. Get a job. Go to college.   Move out. Get a job. Go to college. Move out. Get a job. Go to college. Move out. Get a job.

Move out. Get a job. Go to college.   Move out. Get a job. Go to college. Move out. Get a job. Go to college. Move out. Get a job. Go to college.   Move out. Get a job. Go to college. Move out. Get a job. Go to college. Move out. Get a job. Move out. Get a job. Go to college.   Move out. Get a job. Go to college. Move out. Get a job. Go to college.   Move out. Get a job. Go to college. Move out. Get a job. Go to college. Move out. Get a job.

Move out. Get a job. Go to college.   Move out. Get a job. Go to college. Move out. Get a job. Go to college. Move out. Get a job. Go to college.   Move out. Get a job. Go to college. Move out. Get a job. Go to college. Move out. Get a job.

Move out. Get a job. Go to college.   Move out. Get a job. Go to college. Move out. Get a job. Go to college. Move out. Get a job. Go to college.   Move out. Get a job. Go to college. Move out. Get a job. Go to college. Move out. Get a job.

Move out. Get a job. Go to college.   Move out. Get a job. Go to college. Move out. Get a job. Go to college. Move out. Get a job. Go to college.   Move out. Get a job. Go to college. Move out. Get a job. Go to college. Move out. Get a job.

Move out. Get a job. Go to college.   Move out. Get a job. Go to college. Move out. Get a job. Go to college. Move out. Get a job. Go to college.   Move out. Get a job. Go to college. Move out. Get a job. Go to college. Move out. Get a job. Move out. Get a job. Go to college.   Move out. Get a job. Go to college. Move out. Get a job. Go to college. Move out. Get a job. Go to college.   Move out. Get a job. Go to college. Move out. Get a job. Move out. Get a job. Go to college.   Move out. Get a job. Go to college. Move out. Get a job. Go to college.   Move out. Get a job. Go to college. Move out. Get a job. Go to college.   Move out. Get a job. Move out. Get a job. Go to college.   Move out. Get a job. Go to college. Move out. Get a job. Go to college.   Move out. Get a job. Go to college. Move out. Get a job. Go to college. Move out. Get a job. Move out. Get a job. Go to college.   Move out. Get a job. Go to college. Move out. Get a job. Go to college.   Move out. Get a job. Go to college. Move out. Get a job. Go to college. Move out. Get a job. Go to college.   Move out. Get a job. Go to college. Move out. Get a job. Go to college. Move out. Get a job. Move out. Get a job. Go to college.   Move out. Get a job. Go to college. Move out. Get a job. Go to college. Move out. Get a job. Go to college.   Move out. Get a job. Go to college. Move out. Get a job. Go to college. Move out. Get a job. Move out. Get a job. Go to college.   Move out. Get a job. Go to college. Move out. Get a job. Go

to college. Move out. Get a job. Go to college. Move
out. Get a job. Go to college. Move out. Get a job. Go
to college. Move out. Get a job. Move out. Get a job. Go
to college. Move out. Get a job. Go to college. Move
out. Get a job. Go to college. Move out. Get a job. Go
to college. Move out. Get a job. Go to college. Move
out. Get a job. Go to college. Move out. Get a job. Move
out. Get a job. Go to college. Move out. Get a job. Go
to college. Move out. Get a job. Go to college. Move out.
Get a job. Go to college. Move out. Get a job. Go to
college. Move out. Get a job. Go to college. Move out.
Get a job. Move out. Get a job. Go to college. Move
out. Get a job. Go to college. Move out. Get a job. Go
to college. Move out. Get a job. Go to college. Move
out. Get a job. Go to college. Move out. Get a job. Go
to college. Move out. Get a job. Move out. Get a job. Go
to college. Move out. Get a job. Go to college. Move
out. Get a job. Go to college. Move out. Get a job. Go
to college. Move out. Get a job. Go to college. Move
out. Get a job. Go to college. Move out. Get a job. Move
out. Get a job. Go to college. Move out. Get a job. Go
to college. Move out. Get a job. Go to college. Move out.
Get a job. Go to college. Move out. Get a job. Go to
college. Move out. Get a job. Go to college. Move out.
Get a job. Move out. Get a job. Go to college. Move
out. Get a job. Go to college. Move out. Get a job. Go
to college. Move out. Get a job. Go to college. Move
out. Get a job. Go to college. Move out. Get a job. Go
to college. Move out. Get a job. Move out. Get a job. Go
to college. Move out. Get a job. Go to college. Move
out. Get a job. Go to college. Move out. Get a job. Go
to college. Move out. Get a job. Go to college. Move
out. Get a job. Go to college. Move out. Get a job. Move
out. Get a job. Go to college. Move out. Get a job. Go
to college. Move out. Get a job. Go to college. Move out.
Get a job. Go to college. Move out. Get a job. Go to
college. Move out. Get a job. Go to college. Move out.
Get a job. Move out. Get a job. Go to college. Move

43

out. Get a job. Go to college. Move out. Get a job. Go to college. Move out. Get a job. Go to college. Move out. Get a job. Go to college. Move out. Get a job. Go to college. Move out. Get a job.

Move out. Get a job. Go to college. Move out. Get a job. Go to college. Move out. Get a job. Go to college. Move out. Get a job. Go to college. Move out. Get a job. Go to college. Move out. Get a job. Go to college. Move out. Get a job. Move out. Get a job. Go to college. Move out. Get a job. Go to college. Move out. Get a job. Go to college. Move out. Get a job. Go to college. Move out. Get a job. Go to college. Move out. Get a job. Move out. Get a job. Go to college. Move out. Get a job. Go to college. Move out. Get a job. Go to college. Move out. Get a job. Go to college. Move out. Get a job. Go to college. Move out. Get a job. Move out. Get a job. Go to college. Move out. Get a job. Go to college. Move out. Get a job. Go to college. Move out. Get a job. Go to college. Move out. Get a job. Go to college. Move out. Get a job.

Move out. Get a job. Go to college. Move out. Get a job. Go to college. Move out. Get a job. Go to college. Move out. Get a job. Go to college. Move out. Get a job. Go to college. Move out. Get a job. Go to college. Move out. Get a job. Move out. Get a job. Go to college. Move out. Get a job. Go to college. Move out. Get a job. Go to college. Move out. Get a job. Go to college. Move out. Get a job. Move out. Get a job. Go to college. Move out. Get a job. Go to college. Move out. Get a job. Go to college. Move out. Get a job. Go to college. Move out. Get a job. Move out. Get a job. Go to college. Move out. Get a job. Go to college. Move

out. Get a job. Go to college. Move out. Get a job. Go to college. Move out. Get a job. Move out. Get a job. Go to college. Move out. Get a job. Go to college. Move out. Get a job. Go to college. Move out. Get a job. Go to college. Move out. Get a job. Go to college. Move out. Get a job. Go to college. Move out. Get a job.

Move out. Get a job. Go to college. Move out. Get a job. Go to college. Move out. Get a job. Go to college. Move out. Get a job. Go to college. Move out. Get a job. Go to college. Move out. Get a job. Go to college. Move out. Get a job.

Move out. Get a job. Go to college. Move out. Get a job. Go to college. Move out. Get a job. Go to college. Move out. Get a job. Go to college. Move out. Get a job. Go to college. Move out. Get a job. Go to college. Move out. Get a job.

Move out. Get a job. Go to college. Move out. Get a job. Go to college. Move out. Get a job. Go to college. Move out. Get a job. Go to college. Move out. Get a job. Go to college. Move out. Get a job. Go to college. Move out. Get a job. Go to college. Move out. Get a job. Go to college. Move out. Get a job. Go to college. Move out. Get a job. Go to college. Move out. Get a job. Go to college. Move out. Get a job.

Move out. Get a job. Go to college. Move out. Get a job. Go to college. Move out. Get a job. Go to college. Move out. Get a job. Go to college. Move out. Get a job. Go to college. Move out. Get a job. Go to college. Move out. Get a job. Go to college. Move out. Get a job. Go to college. Move out. Get a job. Go to college. Move out. Get a job. Go to college. Move out. Get a job.

Move out. Get a job. Go to college. Move out. Get a job. Go to college. Move out. Get a job. Go to college.

Move out. Get a job. Go to college.   Move out. Get a job. Go to college. Move out. Get a job. Go to college. Move out. Get a job.

Move out. Get a job. Go to college.   Move out. Get a job. Go to college. Move out. Get a job. Go to college. Move out. Get a job. Go to college.   Move out. Get a job. Go to college. Move out. Get a job. Go to college. Move out. Get a job.

Move out. Get a job. Go to college.   Move out. Get a job. Go to college. Move out. Get a job. Go to college. Move out. Get a job. Go to college.   Move out. Get a job. Go to college. Move out. Get a job. Go to college. Move out. Get a job.

Move out. Get a job. Go to college.   Move out. Get a job. Go to college. Move out. Get a job. Go to college. Move out. Get a job. Go to college.   Move out. Get a job. Go to college. Move out. Get a job. Go to college. Move out. Get a job. Move out. Get a job. Go to college.   Move out. Get a job. Go to college. Move out. Get a job. Go to college. Move out. Get a job. Go to college.   Move out. Get a job. Go to college. Move out. Get a job. Move out. Get a job. Go to college.   Move out. Get a job. Go to college. Move out. Get a job. Go to college. Move out. Get a job. Go to college.   Move out. Get a job. Go to college. Move out. Get a job. Go to college. Move out. Get a job. Move out. Get a job. Go to college.   Move out. Get a job. Go to college. Move out. Get a job. Go to college. Move out. Get a job. Go to college.   Move out. Get a job. Go to college. Move out. Get a job. Go to college. Move out. Get a job. Go to college. Move out. Get a job. Go to college.   Move out. Get a job. Go to college. Move out. Get a job. Go to college.   Move out. Get a job. Go to college. Move out. Get a job. Go to college. Move out. Get a job. Move out. Get a job. Go to college.   Move out. Get a job. Go to college. Move out. Get a job. Go to college. Move out.

Get a job. Go to college. Move out. Get a job. Go to college. Move out. Get a job. Go to college. Move out. Get a job. Move out. Get a job. Go to college. Move out. Get a job. Go to college. Move out. Get a job. Go to college. Move out. Get a job. Go to college. Move out. Get a job. Go to college. Move out. Get a job. Go to college. Move out. Get a job. Move out. Get a job. Go to college. Move out. Get a job. Go to college. Move out. Get a job. Go to college. Move out. Get a job. Go to college. Move out. Get a job. Go to college. Move out. Get a job. Move out. Get a job. Go to college. Move out. Get a job. Go to college. Move out. Get a job. Go to college. Move out. Get a job. Go to college. Move out. Get a job. Go to college. Move out. Get a job. Go to college. Move out. Get a job. Go to college. Move out. Get a job. Move out. Get a job. Go to college. Move out. Get a job. Go to college. Move out. Get a job. Go to college. Move out. Get a job. Go to college. Move out. Get a job. Go to college. Move out. Get a job. Go to college. Move out. Get a job. Go to college. Move out. Get a job. Go to college. Move out. Get a job. Move out. Get a job. Go to college. Move out. Get a job. Go to college. Move out. Get a job. Go to college. Move out. Get a job. Go to college. Move out. Get a job. Go to college. Move out. Get a job. Go to college. Move out. Get a job. Go to college. Move out. Get a job. Move out. Get a job. Go to college. Move out. Get a job. Go to college. Move out. Get a job. Go to college. Move

to college. Move out. Get a job. Go to college. Move out.
Get a job. Go to college. Move out. Get a job. Go to
college. Move out. Get a job. Go to college. Move out.
Get a job. Move out. Get a job. Go to college. Move
out. Get a job. Go to college. Move out. Get a job. Go
to college. Move out. Get a job. Go to college. Move
out. Get a job. Go to college. Move out. Get a job. Go
to college. Move out. Get a job.

Move out. Get a job. Go to college. Move out. Get a
job. Go to college. Move out. Get a job. Go to college.
Move out. Get a job. Go to college. Move out. Get a
job. Go to college. Move out. Get a job. Go to college.
Move out. Get a job. Move out. Get a job. Go to
college. Move out. Get a job. Go to college. Move out.
Get a job. Go to college. Move out. Get a job. Go to
college. Move out. Get a job. Go to college. Move out.
Get a job. Go to college. Move out. Get a job. Move out.
Get a job. Go to college. Move out. Get a job. Go to
college. Move out. Get a job. Go to college. Move out.
Get a job. Go to college. Move out. Get a job. Go to
college. Move out. Get a job. Go to college. Move out.
Get a job. Move out. Get a job. Go to college. Move
out. Get a job. Go to college. Move out. Get a job. Go
to college. Move out. Get a job. Go to college. Move
out. Get a job. Go to college. Move out. Get a job. Go
to college. Move out. Get a job.

Move out. Get a job. Go to college. Move out. Get a
job. Go to college. Move out. Get a job. Go to college.
Move out. Get a job. Go to college. Move out. Get a
job. Go to college. Move out. Get a job. Go to college.
Move out. Get a job. Move out. Get a job. Go to
college. Move out. Get a job. Go to college. Move out.
Get a job. Go to college. Move out. Get a job. Go to
college. Move out. Get a job. Go to college. Move out.
Get a job. Go to college. Move out. Get a job. Move out.
Get a job. Go to college. Move out. Get a job. Go to
college. Move out. Get a job. Go to college. Move out.
Get a job. Go to college. Move out. Get a job. Go to

college. Move out. Get a job. Go to college. Move out. Get a job. Move out. Get a job. Go to college.   Move out. Get a job. Go to college. Move out. Get a job. Go to college. Move out. Get a job. Go to college.   Move out. Get a job. Go to college. Move out. Get a job. Go to college. Move out. Get a job. Move out. Get a job. Go to college.   Move out. Get a job. Go to college. Move out. Get a job. Go to college.   Move out. Get a job. Go to college. Move out. Get a job. Go to college. Move out. Get a job. Go to college. Move out. Get a job.

Move out. Get a job. Go to college.   Move out. Get a job. Go to college. Move out. Get a job. Go to college. Move out. Get a job. Go to college.   Move out. Get a job. Go to college. Move out. Get a job. Go to college. Move out. Get a job.

Move out. Get a job. Go to college.   Move out. Get a job. Go to college. Move out. Get a job. Go to college. Move out. Get a job. Go to college.   Move out. Get a job. Go to college. Move out. Get a job. Go to college. Move out. Get a job.

Move out. Get a job. Go to college.   Move out. Get a job. Go to college. Move out. Get a job. Go to college. Move out. Get a job. Go to college.   Move out. Get a job. Go to college.   Move out. Get a job. Go to college. Move out. Get a job. Go to college. Move out. Get a job. Go to college. Move out. Get a job. Go to college.   Move out. Get a job. Go to college. Move out. Get a job. Go to college. Move out. Get a job.

Move out. Get a job. Go to college.   Move out. Get a job. Go to college. Move out. Get a job. Go to college. Move out. Get a job. Go to college.   Move out. Get a job. Go to college. Move out. Get a job. Go to college. Move out. Get a job. Move out. Get a job. Go to college.   Move out. Get a job. Go to college. Move out. Get a job. Go to college. Move out. Get a job. Go to college. Move out. Get a job. Go to college. Move out. Get a job. Go to college. Move out. Get a job.

Move out. Get a job. Go to college. Move out. Get a job. Go to college. Move out. Get a job. Go to college. Move out. Get a job. Go to college. Move out. Get a job. Go to college. Move out. Get a job. Go to college. Move out. Get a job.

Move out. Get a job. Go to college. Move out. Get a job. Go to college. Move out. Get a job. Go to college. Move out. Get a job. Go to college. Move out. Get a job. Go to college. Move out. Get a job. Go to college. Move out. Get a job.

Move out. Get a job. Go to college. Move out. Get a job. Go to college. Move out. Get a job. Go to college. Move out. Get a job. Go to college. Move out. Get a job. Go to college. Move out. Get a job. Go to college. Move out. Get a job.

Move out. Get a job. Go to college. Move out. Get a job. Go to college. Move out. Get a job. Go to college. Move out. Get a job. Go to college. Move out. Get a job. Go to college. Move out. Get a job. Go to college. Move out. Get a job. Move out. Get a job. Go to college. Move out. Get a job. Go to college. Move out. Get a job. Go to college. Move out. Get a job. Go to college. Move out. Get a job. Go to college. Move out. Get a job. Move out. Get a job. Go to college. Move out. Get a job. Go to college. Move out. Get a job. Go to college. Move out. Get a job. Go to college. Move out. Get a job. Go to college. Move out. Get a job. Go to college. Move out. Get a job. Move out. Get a job. Go to college. Move out. Get a job. Go to college. Move out. Get a job. Go to college. Move out. Get a job. Go to college. Move out. Get a job. Move out. Get a job. Go to college. Move out. Get a job. Go to college. Move out. Get a job. Go to college. Move out. Get a job. Go to college. Move out. Get a job. Go to college. Move out. Get a job. Go to college. Move out. Get a job. Go to college. Move out. Get a job. Move out. Get a job. Go to college. Move out. Get a job. Go to college. Move out. Get a job. Go to college. Move out. Get a job. Go to college. Move out. Get a job. Go to college. Move out. Get a job. Go to college. Move out. Get a job. Move out. Get a job. Go to college. Move out. Get a job. Go to college. Move out. Get a job. Go to college. Move out. Get a job. Go to college. Move out. Get a job. Go to college. Move out. Get a job. Move out. Get a job. Go to college. Move out. Get a job. Go to college. Move out. Get a job. Go to college. Move out. Get a job. Go to college. Move out. Get a job. Move out. Get a job. Go to college. Move out. Get a job. Go to college. Move out. Get a job. Go to college. Move out. Get a job. Go to college. Move out. Get a job. Go to college. Move out. Get a job. Go to college. Move out. Get a job. Move out. Get a job. Go to college. Move out. Get a job. Go to college. Move out. Get a job. Go to college. Move out. Get a job. Go to college. Move out. Get a job. Go to college. Move out. Get a job. Go to college. Move out. Get a job. Go to college. Move out. Get a job. Go to college. Move out. Get a job. Move out. Get a job. Go to college. Move out. Get a job. Go to college. Move out. Get a job. Go to college. Move out. Get a job. Go to college. Move out. Get a job. Go to college. Move out. Get a job. Move out. Get a job. Go to college. Move out. Get a job. Go to college. Move out. Get a job. Go to college. Move out. Get a job. Go to college. Move out. Get a job. Go to college. Move out. Get a job. Move out. Get a job. Go to college. Move out. Get a job. Go to college. Move out. Get a job. Go to college.   Move out. Get a job. Go to college. Move out. Get a job. Go to college. Move out. Get a job. Move out. Get a job. Go to college.   Move out. Get a job. Go to college. Move out. Get a job. Go to college. Move out. Get a job. Go to college. Move out. Get a job. Go to college.   Move out. Get a job. Go to college. Move out. Get a job. Go to college. Move out. Get a job. Move out. Get a job. Go to college.   Move out. Get a job. Go to college. Move out. Get a job. Go to college. Move out. Get a job. Go to college.   Move out. Get a job. Go to college. Move out. Get a job. Go to college. Move out. Get a job.

Move out. Get a job. Go to college.   Move out. Get a job. Go to college. Move out. Get a job. Go to college. Move out. Get a job. Go to college.   Move out. Get a job. Go to college. Move out. Get a job. Go to college. Move out. Get a job. Move out. Get a job. Go to college.   Move out. Get a job. Go to college. Move out. Get a job. Go to college. Move out. Get a job. Go to college. Move out. Get a job. Go to college. Move out. Get a job. Move out. Get a job. Go to college.   Move out. Get a job. Go to college. Move out. Get a job. Go to college.   Move out. Get a job. Go to college. Move out. Get a job. Go to college. Move out. Get a job. Move out. Get a job. Go to college.   Move out. Get a job. Go to college. Move out. Get a job. Go to collegc. Move out. Get a job. Go to college.   Move out. Get a job. Go to college. Move out. Get a job. Go to college. Move out. Get a job.

Move out. Get a job. Go to college.   Move out. Get a job. Go to college. Move out. Get a job. Go to college. Move out. Get a job. Go to college.   Move out. Get a job. Go to college. Move out. Get a job. Go to college. Move out. Get a job. Move out. Get a job. Go to college.   Move out. Get a job. Go to college. Move out. Get a job. Go to college. Move out. Get a job. Go to college.   Move out. Get a job. Go to college. Move out.

Get a job. Go to college. Move out. Get a job. Move out.
Get a job. Go to college.   Move out. Get a job. Go to
college. Move out. Get a job. Go to college. Move out.
Get a job. Go to college.   Move out. Get a job. Go to
college. Move out. Get a job. Go to college. Move out.
Get a job. Move out. Get a job. Go to college.   Move
out. Get a job. Go to college. Move out. Get a job. Go
to college. Move out. Get a job. Go to college.   Move
out. Get a job. Go to college. Move out. Get a job. Go
to college. Move out. Get a job. Move out. Get a job. Go
to college.   Move out. Get a job. Go to college. Move
out. Get a job. Go to college. Move out. Get a job. Go
to college.   Move out. Get a job. Go to college. Move
out. Get a job. Go to college. Move out. Get a job.

Move out. Get a job. Go to college.   Move out. Get a
job. Go to college. Move out. Get a job. Go to college.
Move out. Get a job. Go to college.   Move out. Get a
job. Go to college. Move out. Get a job. Go to college.
Move out. Get a job.

Move out. Get a job. Go to college.   Move out. Get a
job. Go to college. Move out. Get a job. Go to college.
Move out. Get a job. Go to college.   Move out. Get a
job. Go to college. Move out. Get a job. Go to college.
Move out. Get a job.

Move out. Get a job. Go to college.   Move out. Get a
job. Go to college. Move out. Get a job. Go to college.
Move out. Get a job. Go to college.   Move out. Get a
job. Go to college. Move out. Get a job. Go to college.
Move out. Get a job. Move out. Get a job. Go to
college.   Move out. Get a job. Go to college. Move out.
Get a job. Go to college. Move out. Get a job. Go to
college.   Move out. Get a job. Go to college. Move out.
Get a job. Go to college. Move out. Get a job.

Move out. Get a job. Go to college.   Move out. Get a
job. Go to college. Move out. Get a job. Go to college.
Move out. Get a job. Go to college.   Move out. Get a
job. Go to college. Move out. Get a job. Go to college.

Move out. Get a job. Move out. Get a job. Go to college. Move out. Get a job. Go to college. Move out. Get a job. Go to college. Move out. Get a job. Go to college. Move out. Get a job. Go to college. Move out. Get a job. Go to college. Move out. Get a job.

Move out. Get a job. Go to college. Move out. Get a job. Go to college. Move out. Get a job. Go to college. Move out. Get a job. Go to college. Move out. Get a job. Go to college. Move out. Get a job. Go to college. Move out. Get a job.

Move out. Get a job. Go to college. Move out. Get a job. Go to college. Move out. Get a job. Go to college. Move out. Get a job. Go to college. Move out. Get a job. Go to college. Move out. Get a job. Go to college. Move out. Get a job.

Move out. Get a job. Go to college. Move out. Get a job. Go to college. Move out. Get a job. Go to college. Move out. Get a job. Go to college. Move out. Get a job. Go to college. Move out. Get a job. Go to college. Move out. Get a job.

Move out. Get a job. Go to college. Move out. Get a job. Go to college. Move out. Get a job. Go to college. Move out. Get a job. Go to college. Move out. Get a job. Go to college. Move out. Get a job. Go to college. Move out. Get a job. Move out. Get a job. Go to college. Move out. Get a job. Go to college. Move out. Get a job. Go to college. Move out. Get a job. Go to college. Move out. Get a job. Go to college. Move out. Get a job. Move out. Get a job. Go to college. Move out. Get a job. Go to college. Move out. Get a job. Go to college. Move out. Get a job. Go to college. Move out. Get a job. Go to college. Move out. Get a job. Go to college. Move out. Get a job. Move out. Get a job. Go to college. Move out. Get a job. Go to college. Move out. Get a job. Go to college. Move out. Get a job. Go to college. Move out. Get a job. Go to college. Move out. Get a job. Go to college. Move out. Get a job. Move out. Get a job. Go to college. Move out. Get a job. Go to college. Move out. Get a job. Go to college. Move out. Get a job. Go to college. Move out. Get a job. Go to college. Move out. Get a job. Go to college. Move out. Get a job. Move out. Get a job. Go to college. Move out. Get a job. Go to college. Move out. Get a job. Go to college. Move out. Get a job. Go to college. Move out. Get a job. Go to college. Move out. Get a job. Move out. Get a job. Go to college. Move out. Get a job. Go to college. Move out. Get a job. Go to college. Move out. Get a job. Go to college. Move out. Get a job. Go to college. Move out. Get a job. Move out. Get a job. Go to college. Move out. Get a job. Go to college. Move out. Get a job. Go to college. Move out. Get a job. Go to college. Move out. Get a job. Go to college. Move out. Get a job. Move out. Get a job. Go to college. Move out. Get a job. Go to college. Move out. Get a job. Go to college. Move out. Get a job. Go to college. Move out. Get a job. Go to college. Move out. Get a job. Move out. Get a job. Go to college. Move out. Get a job. Go to college. Move out. Get a job. Go to college. Move out. Get a job. Go to college. Move out. Get a job. Go to college. Move out. Get a job. Move out. Get a job. Go to college. Move out. Get a job. Go to college. Move out. Get a job. Go to college. Move out. Get a job. Go to college. Move out. Get a job. Go to college. Move out. Get a job. Go to college. Move out. Get a job. Move out. Get a job. Go to college.   Move out. Get a job. Go to college. Move out. Get a job. Go to college. Move out. Get a job. Go to college.   Move out. Get a job. Go to college. Move out. Get a job. Go to college. Move out. Get a job. Move out. Get a job. Go to college.   Move out. Get a job. Go to college. Move out. Get a job. Go to college. Move out. Get a job. Go to college. Move out. Get a job. Go to college.   Move out. Get a job. Go to college.   Move out. Get a job. Go to college. Move out. Get a job. Move out. Get a job. Go to college.   Move out. Get a job. Go to college. Move out. Get a job. Go to college.   Move out. Get a job. Go to college. Move out. Get a job. Go to college. Move out. Get a job.

Move out. Get a job. Go to college.   Move out. Get a job. Go to college. Move out. Get a job. Go to college. Move out. Get a job. Go to college.   Move out. Get a job. Go to college. Move out. Get a job. Go to college. Move out. Get a job. Move out. Get a job. Go to college.   Move out. Get a job. Go to college. Move out. Get a job. Go to college.   Move out. Get a job. Go to college. Move out. Get a job. Go to college. Move out. Get a job. Go to college. Move out. Get a job.   Move out. Get a job. Go to college. Move out. Get a job. Go to college. Move out. Get a job. Go to college.   Move out. Get a job. Go to college. Move out. Get a job. Go to college. Move out. Get a job. Move out. Get a job. Go to college.   Move out. Get a job. Go to college. Move out. Get a job. Go to college.   Move out. Get a job. Go to college. Move out. Get a job. Go to college. Move out. Get a job.

Move out. Get a job. Go to college.   Move out. Get a job. Go to college. Move out. Get a job. Go to college. Move out. Get a job. Go to college.   Move out. Get a job. Go to college. Move out. Get a job. Go to college. Move out. Get a job. Move out. Get a job. Go to

college. Move out. Get a job. Go to college. Move out.
 Get a job. Go to college. Move out. Get a job. Go to
college. Move out. Get a job. Go to college. Move out.
Get a job. Go to college. Move out. Get a job. Move out.
 Get a job. Go to college.   Move out. Get a job. Go to
college. Move out. Get a job. Go to college. Move out.
 Get a job. Go to college.   Move out. Get a job. Go to
college. Move out. Get a job. Go to college. Move out.
 Get a job. Move out. Get a job. Go to college.   Move
out. Get a job. Go to college. Move out. Get a job. Go
to college. Move out. Get a job. Go to college.   Move
out. Get a job. Go to college. Move out. Get a job. Go
to college. Move out. Get a job. Move out. Get a job. Go
to college.   Move out. Get a job. Go to college. Move
out. Get a job. Go to college. Move out. Get a job. Go
to college.   Move out. Get a job. Go to college. Move
 out. Get a job. Go to college. Move out. Get a job.

Move out. Get a job. Go to college.   Move out. Get a
job. Go to college. Move out. Get a job. Go to college.
Move out. Get a job. Go to college.   Move out. Get a
job. Go to college. Move out. Get a job. Go to college.
Move out. Get a job.

Move out. Get a job. Go to college.   Move out. Get a
job. Go to college. Move out. Get a job. Go to college.
Move out. Get a job. Go to college.   Move out. Get a
job. Go to college. Move out. Get a job. Go to college.
Move out. Get a job.

Move out. Get a job. Go to college.   Move out. Get a
job. Go to college. Move out. Get a job. Go to college.
Move out. Get a job. Go to college.   Move out. Get a
job. Go to college. Move out. Get a job. Go to college.
 Move out. Get a job. Move out. Get a job. Go to
college.   Move out. Get a job. Go to college. Move out.
 Get a job. Go to college. Move out. Get a job. Go to
college.   Move out. Get a job. Go to college. Move out.
  Get a job. Go to college. Move out. Get a job.

Move out. Get a job. Go to college.   Move out. Get a job. Go to college. Move out. Get a job. Go to college. Move out. Get a job. Go to college.   Move out. Get a job. Go to college. Move out. Get a job. Go to college. Move out. Get a job. Move out. Get a job. Go to college.   Move out. Get a job. Go to college. Move out. Get a job. Go to college. Move out. Get a job. Go to college.   Move out. Get a job. Go to college. Move out. Get a job. Go to college. Move out. Get a job.

Move out. Get a job. Go to college.   Move out. Get a job. Go to college. Move out. Get a job. Go to college. Move out. Get a job. Go to college.   Move out. Get a job. Go to college. Move out. Get a job. Go to college. Move out. Get a job.

Move out. Get a job. Go to college.   Move out. Get a job. Go to college. Move out. Get a job. Go to college. Move out. Get a job. Go to college.   Move out. Get a job. Go to college. Move out. Get a job. Go to college. Move out. Get a job.

Move out. Get a job. Go to college.   Move out. Get a job. Go to college. Move out. Get a job. Go to college.   Move out. Get a job. Go to college. Move out. Get a job. Go to college. Move out. Get a job.

Move out. Get a job. Go to college.   Move out. Get a job. Go to college. Move out. Get a job. Go to college.   Move out. Get a job. Go to college. Move out. Get a job. Go to college. Move out. Get a job. Move out. Get a job. Go to college.   Move out. Get a job. Go to college. Move out. Get a job. Go to college. Move out. Get a job. Go to college.   Move out. Get a job. Go to college. Move out. Get a job. Go to college. Move out. Get a job. Go to college. Move out. Get a job. Go to college.   Move out. Get a job. Go to college. Move out. Get a job. Go to college. Move out. Get a job. Go to college.   Move out. Get a job. Go to college. Move out. Get a job. Go to college. Move out.

Get a job. Move out. Get a job. Go to college. Move out. Get a job. Go to college. Move out. Get a job. Go to college. Move out. Get a job. Go to college. Move out. Get a job. Go to college. Move out. Get a job. Go to college. Move out. Get a job. Move out. Get a job. Go to college. Move out. Get a job. Go to college. Move out. Get a job. Go to college. Move out. Get a job. Go to college. Move out. Get a job. Go to college. Move out. Get a job. Move out. Get a job. Go to college. Move out. Get a job. Go to college. Move out. Get a job. Go to college. Move out. Get a job. Go to college. Move out. Get a job. Go to college. Move out. Get a job. Go to college. Move out. Get a job. Go to college. Move out. Get a job. Go to college. Move out. Get a job. Go to college. Move out. Get a job. Go to college. Move out. Get a job. Move out. Get a job. Go to college. Move out. Get a job. Go to college. Move out. Get a job. Go to college. Move out. Get a job. Go to college. Move out. Get a job. Go to college. Move out. Get a job. Go to college. Move out. Get a job. Go to college. Move out. Get a job. Go to college. Move out. Get a job. Move out. Get a job. Go to college. Move out. Get a job. Go to college. Move out. Get a job. Go to college. Move out. Get a job. Go to college. Move out. Get a job. Go to college. Move out. Get a job. Go to college. Move out. Get a job. Go to college. Move out. Get a job. Go to college. Move out. Get a job. Move out. Get a job. Go to college. Move out. Get a job. Go to college. Move out. Get a job. Go to college. Move out. Get a job. Go to college. Move out. Get a job. Go to college. Move out. Get a job. Go to college. Move out. Get a job. Go to college. Move out. Get a job. Go to college. Move out. Get a job. Go to college. Move out. Get a job. Go to college. Move out. Get a job. Go to college. Move out. Get a job. Move out. Get a job. Go to college. Move out. Get a job. Go to college. Move out. Get a job. Go to college. Move out. Get a job. Go to college. Move out. Get a job. Go to college. Move out. Get a job. Go to college. Move out. Get a job. Move out. Get a job. Go to college. Move out. Get a job. Go to college. Move out. Get a job. Go to college. Move out. Get a job. Go to college. Move out. Get a job. Move out. Get a job. Go to college. Move out. Get a job. Go to college. Move out. Get a job. Go to college. Move out. Get a job. Go to college. Move out. Get a job. Go to college. Move out. Get a job. Go to college. Move out. Get a job. Move out. Get a job. Go to college. Move out. Get a job. Go to college. Move out. Get a job. Go to college. Move out. Get a job. Go to college. Move out. Get a job. Go to college. Move out. Get a job.

Move out. Get a job. Go to college. Move out. Get a job. Go to college. Move out. Get a job. Go to college. Move out. Get a job. Go to college. Move out. Get a job. Go to college. Move out. Get a job. Move out. Get a job. Go to college. Move out. Get a job. Go to college. Move out. Get a job. Go to college. Move out. Get a job. Go to college. Move out. Get a job. Go to college. Move out. Get a job. Go to college. Move out. Get a job. Go to college. Move out. Get a job. Go to college. Move out. Get a job. Go to college. Move out. Get a job. Move out. Get a job. Go to college. Move out. Get a job. Go to college. Move out. Get a job. Go to college. Move out. Get a job. Go to college. Move out. Get a job.

Move out. Get a job. Go to college. Move out. Get a job. Go to college. Move out. Get a job. Go to college. Move out. Get a job. Go to college. Move out. Get a job. Go to college. Move out. Get a job. Go to college. Move out. Get a job. Move out. Get a job. Go to college. Move out. Get a job. Go to college. Move out. Get a job. Go to college. Move out. Get a job. Go to college. Move out. Get a job. Go to college. Move out. Get a job. Go to college. Move out. Get a job. Move out. Get a job. Go to college. Move out. Get a job. Go to college. Move out. Get a job. Go to college. Move out. Get a job. Go to college. Move out. Get a job. Move out. Get a job. Go to college. Move out. Get a job. Go to college. Move out. Get a job. Go to college. Move out. Get a job. Go to college. Move out. Get a job. Go to college. Move out. Get a job. Go to college. Move out. Get a job. Go to college. Move out. Get a job. Go to college. Move out. Get a job. Go to college. Move out. Get a job.

Move out. Get a job. Go to college. Move out. Get a job. Go to college. Move out. Get a job. Go to college. Move out. Get a job. Go to college. Move out. Get a job. Go to college. Move out. Get a job. Go to college. Move out. Get a job.

Move out. Get a job. Go to college. Move out. Get a job. Go to college. Move out. Get a job. Go to college. Move out. Get a job. Go to college. Move out. Get a job. Go to college. Move out. Get a job.

Move out. Get a job. Go to college. Move out. Get a job. Go to college. Move out. Get a job. Go to college. Move out. Get a job. Go to college. Move out. Get a job. Move out. Get a job. Go to

61

college. Move out. Get a job. Go to college. Move out. Get a job. Go to college. Move out. Get a job. Go to college. Move out. Get a job. Go to college. Move out. Get a job. Go to college. Move out. Get a job.

Move out. Get a job. Go to college. Move out. Get a job. Go to college. Move out. Get a job. Go to college. Move out. Get a job. Go to college. Move out. Get a job. Go to college. Move out. Get a job. Go to college. Move out. Get a job. Move out. Get a job. Go to college. Move out. Get a job. Go to college. Move out. Get a job. Go to college. Move out. Get a job. Go to college. Move out. Get a job. Go to college. Move out. Get a job.

Move out. Get a job. Go to college. Move out. Get a job. Go to college. Move out. Get a job. Go to college. Move out. Get a job. Go to college. Move out. Get a job. Go to college. Move out. Get a job.

Move out. Get a job. Go to college. Move out. Get a job. Go to college. Move out. Get a job. Go to college. Move out. Get a job. Go to college. Move out. Get a job. Go to college. Move out. Get a job.

Move out. Get a job. Go to college. Move out. Get a job. Go to college. Move out. Get a job. Go to college. Move out. Get a job. Go to college. Move out. Get a job. Go to college. Move out. Get a job.

Move out. Get a job. Go to college. Move out. Get a job. Go to college. Move out. Get a job. Go to college. Move out. Get a job. Go to college. Move out. Get a job. Move out. Get a job. Go to college. Move out. Get a job. Go to college. Move out. Get a job. Go to college. Move out. Get a job. Go to college. Move out.

Get a job. Go to college. Move out. Get a job. Move out. Get a job. Go to college. Move out. Get a job. Go to college. Move out. Get a job. Go to college. Move out. Get a job. Go to college. Move out. Get a job. Go to college. Move out. Get a job. Go to college. Move out. Get a job. Move out. Get a job. Go to college. Move out. Get a job. Go to college. Move out. Get a job. Go to college. Move out. Get a job. Go to college. Move out. Get a job. Go to college. Move out. Get a job. Go to college. Move out. Get a job. Move out. Get a job. Go to college. Move out. Get a job. Go to college. Move out. Get a job. Go to college. Move out. Get a job. Go to college. Move out. Get a job. Go to college. Move out. Get a job. Move out. Get a job. Go to college. Move out. Get a job. Go to college. Move out. Get a job. Go to college. Move out. Get a job. Go to college. Move out. Get a job. Go to college. Move out. Get a job. Go to college. Move out. Get a job. Move out. Get a job. Go to college. Move out. Get a job. Go to college. Move out. Get a job. Go to college. Move out. Get a job. Go to college. Move out. Get a job. Go to college. Move out. Get a job. Go to college. Move out. Get a job. Move out. Get a job. Go to college. Move out. Get a job. Go to college. Move out. Get a job. Go to college. Move out. Get a job. Move out. Get a job. Go to college. Move out. Get a job. Go to college. Move out. Get a job. Go to college. Move out. Get a job. Go

63

to college. Move out. Get a job. Go to college. Move out. Get a job. Go to college. Move out. Get a job. Move out. Get a job. Go to college. Move out. Get a job. Go to college. Move out. Get a job. Go to college. Move out. Get a job. Go to college. Move out. Get a job. Go to college. Move out. Get a job. Go to college. Move out. Get a job. Move out. Get a job. Go to college. Move out. Get a job. Go to college. Move out. Get a job. Go to college. Move out. Get a job. Go to college. Move out. Get a job. Go to college. Move out. Get a job. Move out. Get a job. Go to college. Move out. Get a job. Go to college. Move out. Get a job. Go to college. Move out. Get a job. Go to college. Move out. Get a job. Go to college. Move out. Get a job. Move out. Get a job. Go to college. Move out. Get a job. Go to college. Move out. Get a job. Go to college. Move out. Get a job. Go to college. Move out. Get a job. Move out. Get a job. Go to college. Move out. Get a job. Go to college. Move out. Get a job. Go to college. Move out. Get a job. Go to college. Move out. Get a job. Go to college. Move out. Get a job.

Move out. Get a job. Go to college. Move out. Get a job. Go to college. Move out. Get a job. Go to college. Move out. Get a job. Go to college. Move out. Get a job. Go to college. Move out. Get a job. Go to college. Move out. Get a job. Move out. Get a job. Go to college. Move out. Get a job. Go to college. Move out. Get a job. Go to college. Move out. Get a job. Go to college. Move out. Get a job. Move out. Get a job. Go to college. Move out. Get a job. Go to college. Move out. Get a job. Go to college. Move out. Get a job. Go to college. Move out. Get a job. Move out. Get a job. Go to college. Move

64

out. Get a job. Go to college. Move out. Get a job. Go to college. Move out. Get a job. Go to college.   Move out. Get a job. Go to college. Move out. Get a job. Go to college. Move out. Get a job.

Move out. Get a job. Go to college.   Move out. Get a job. Go to college. Move out. Get a job. Go to college. Move out. Get a job. Go to college.   Move out. Get a job. Go to college. Move out. Get a job. Go to college. Move out. Get a job. Move out. Get a job. Go to college. Move out. Get a job. Go to college. Move out. Get a job. Go to college. Move out. Get a job. Go to college. Move out. Get a job. Go to college. Move out. Get a job. Go to college. Move out. Get a job. Move out. Get a job. Go to college.   Move out. Get a job. Go to college. Move out. Get a job. Go to college. Move out. Get a job. Go to college.   Move out. Get a job. Go to college. Move out. Get a job. Go to college. Move out. Get a job. Move out. Get a job. Go to college.   Move out. Get a job. Go to college. Move out. Get a job. Go to college.   Move out. Get a job. Go to college. Move out. Get a job. Go to college. Move out. Get a job. Go to college.   Move out. Get a job. Go to college. Move out. Get a job. Go to college.   Move out. Get a job. Go to college. Move out. Get a job.

Move out. Get a job. Go to college.   Move out. Get a job. Go to college. Move out. Get a job. Go to college. Move out. Get a job. Go to college.   Move out. Get a job. Go to college. Move out. Get a job. Go to college. Move out. Get a job.

Move out. Get a job. Go to college.   Move out. Get a job. Go to college. Move out. Get a job. Go to college. Move out. Get a job. Go to college.   Move out. Get a job. Go to college. Move out. Get a job. Go to college. Move out. Get a job.

Move out. Get a job. Go to college.   Move out. Get a job. Go to college. Move out. Get a job. Go to college. Move out. Get a job. Go to college.   Move out. Get a job. Go to college. Move out. Get a job. Go to college. Move out. Get a job. Move out. Get a job. Go to college.   Move out. Get a job. Go to college. Move out. Get a job. Go to college. Move out. Get a job. Go to college.   Move out. Get a job. Go to college. Move out. Get a job.

Move out. Get a job. Go to college.   Move out. Get a job. Go to college. Move out. Get a job. Go to college. Move out. Get a job. Go to college.   Move out. Get a job. Go to college. Move out. Get a job. Go to college. Move out. Get a job. Move out. Get a job. Go to college.   Move out. Get a job. Go to college. Move out. Get a job. Go to college. Move out. Get a job. Go to college.   Move out. Get a job. Go to college. Move out. Get a job.

Move out. Get a job. Go to college.   Move out. Get a job. Go to college. Move out. Get a job. Go to college. Move out. Get a job. Go to college.   Move out. Get a job. Go to college. Move out. Get a job. Go to college. Move out. Get a job.

Move out. Get a job. Go to college.   Move out. Get a job. Go to college. Move out. Get a job. Go to college. Move out. Get a job. Go to college.   Move out. Get a job. Go to college. Move out. Get a job. Go to college. Move out. Get a job.

Move out. Get a job. Go to college.   Move out. Get a job. Go to college. Move out. Get a job. Go to college.   Move out. Get a job. Go to college. Move out. Get a job. Go to college. Move out. Get a job.

Move out. Get a job. Go to college.   Move out. Get a job. Go to college. Move out. Get a job. Go to college.   Move out. Get a

job. Go to college. Move out. Get a job. Go to college. Move out. Get a job. Move out. Get a job. Go to college. Move out. Get a job. Go to college. Move out. Get a job. Go to college. Move out. Get a job. Go to college. Move out. Get a job. Go to college. Move out. Get a job. Go to college. Move out. Get a job. Move out. Get a job. Go to college. Move out. Get a job. Go to college. Move out. Get a job. Go to college. Move out. Get a job. Go to college. Move out. Get a job. Go to college. Move out. Get a job. Move out. Get a job. Go to college. Move out. Get a job. Go to college. Move out. Get a job. Go to college. Move out. Get a job. Go to college. Move out. Get a job. Move out. Get a job. Go to college. Move out. Get a job. Go to college. Move out. Get a job. Go to college. Move out. Get a job. Go to college. Move out. Get a job. Go to college. Move out. Get a job. Move out. Get a job. Go to college. Move out. Get a job. Go to college. Move out. Get a job. Go to college. Move out. Get a job. Go to college. Move out. Get a job. Move out. Get a job. Go to college. Move out. Get a job. Go to college. Move out. Get a job. Go to college. Move out. Get a job. Go to college. Move out. Get a job. Go to college. Move out. Get a job. Move out. Get a job. Go to college. Move out. Get a job. Go to college. Move out. Get a job. Go to college. Move out. Get a job. Go to college. Move out. Get a job. Move out. Get a job. Go to college. Move out. Get a job. Go to college. Move out. Get a job. Go to college. Move out. Get a job. Go to college. Move out. Get a job. Go to college. Move out. Get a job. Move out. Get a job. Go to college. Move out. Get a job. Go to college. Move out. Get a job. Go to college. Move out. Get a job. Go to college. Move out. Get a job. Go to college. Move out. Get a job. Move out. Get a job. Go to college. Move out. Get a job. Go to college. Move out. Get a job. Go to college. Move out. Get a job. Go to college. Move out. Get a job. Go to college. Move out. Get a job. Move out. Get a job. Go to college. Move out. Get a job. Go to college. Move out. Get a job. Go to college. Move out. Get a job. Go to college. Move out. Get a job. Go to college. Move out. Get a job. Go to college. Move out. Get a job. Move out. Get a job. Go to college. Move out. Get a job. Go to college. Move out. Get a job. Go to college. Move out. Get a job. Go to college. Move out. Get a job. Go to college. Move out. Get a job. Go to college. Move out. Get a job. Go to college. Move out. Get a job. Move out. Get a job. Go to college. Move out. Get a job. Go to college. Move out. Get a job. Go to college. Move out. Get a job. Go to college. Move out. Get a job. Go to college. Move out. Get a job. Move out. Get a job. Go to college. Move out. Get a job. Go to college. Move out. Get a job. Go to college. Move out. Get a job. Go to college. Move out. Get a job.

Move out. Get a job. Go to college. Move out. Get a job. Go to college. Move out. Get a job. Go to college. Move out. Get a job. Go to college. Move out. Get a job. Go to college. Move out. Get a job. Go to college. Move out. Get a job. Move out. Get a job. Go to college. Move out. Get a job. Go to college. Move out. Get a job. Go to college. Move out. Get a job. Go to college. Move out. Get a job. Go to college. Move out. Get a job. Move out.

Get a job. Go to college. Move out. Get a job. Go to college. Move out. Get a job. Go to college. Move out. Get a job. Go to college. Move out. Get a job. Go to college. Move out. Get a job. Go to college. Move out. Get a job. Move out. Get a job. Go to college. Move out. Get a job. Go to college. Move out. Get a job. Go to college. Move out. Get a job. Go to college. Move out. Get a job. Go to college. Move out. Get a job.

Move out. Get a job. Go to college. Move out. Get a job. Go to college. Move out. Get a job. Go to college. Move out. Get a job. Go to college. Move out. Get a job. Go to college. Move out. Get a job. Move out. Get a job. Go to college. Move out. Get a job. Go to college. Move out. Get a job. Go to college. Move out. Get a job. Go to college. Move out. Get a job. Go to college. Move out. Get a job. Move out. Get a job. Go to college. Move out. Get a job. Go to college. Move out. Get a job. Go to college. Move out. Get a job. Go to college. Move out. Get a job. Move out. Get a job. Go to college. Move out. Get a job. Go to college. Move out. Get a job. Go to college. Move out. Get a job. Go to college. Move out. Get a job. Go to college. Move out. Get a job. Go to college. Move out. Get a job. Go to college. Move out. Get a job.

Move out. Get a job. Go to college. Move out. Get a job. Go to college. Move out. Get a job. Go to college. Move out. Get a job. Go to college. Move out. Get a job. Go to college. Move out. Get a job. Go to college. Move out. Get a job.

69

Move out. Get a job. Go to college.   Move out. Get a job. Go to college. Move out. Get a job. Go to college. Move out. Get a job. Go to college.   Move out. Get a job. Go to college. Move out. Get a job. Go to college. Move out. Get a job.

Move out. Get a job. Go to college.   Move out. Get a job. Go to college. Move out. Get a job. Go to college. Move out. Get a job. Go to college.   Move out. Get a job. Go to college. Move out. Get a job. Go to college. Move out. Get a job. Move out. Get a job. Go to college.   Move out. Get a job. Go to college. Move out. Get a job. Go to college. Move out. Get a job. Go to college.   Move out. Get a job. Go to college. Move out. Get a job.

Move out. Get a job. Go to college.   Move out. Get a job. Go to college. Move out. Get a job. Go to college. Move out. Get a job. Go to college.   Move out. Get a job. Go to college. Move out. Get a job. Go to college. Move out. Get a job. Move out. Get a job. Go to college.   Move out. Get a job. Go to college. Move out. Get a job. Go to college. Move out. Get a job. Go to college.   Move out. Get a job. Go to college. Move out. Get a job.

Move out. Get a job. Go to college.   Move out. Get a job. Go to college. Move out. Get a job. Go to college. Move out. Get a job. Go to college.   Move out. Get a job. Go to college. Move out. Get a job. Go to college. Move out. Get a job.

Move out. Get a job. Go to college.   Move out. Get a job. Go to college. Move out. Get a job. Go to college. Move out. Get a job. Go to college.   Move out. Get a job. Go to college. Move out. Get a job. Go to college. Move out. Get a job.

Move out. Get a job. Go to college.   Move out. Get a job. Go to college. Move out. Get a job. Go to college.   Move out. Get a

job. Go to college. Move out. Get a job. Go to college. Move out. Get a job.

Move out. Get a job. Go to college.   Move out. Get a job. Go to college. Move out. Get a job. Go to college. Move out. Get a job. Go to college.   Move out. Get a job. Go to college. Move out. Get a job. Go to college. Move out. Get a job. Move out. Get a job. Go to college.   Move out. Get a job. Go to college. Move out. Get a job. Go to college. Move out. Get a job. Go to college.   Move out. Get a job. Go to college. Move out. Get a job. Move out. Get a job. Go to college.   Move out. Get a job. Go to college. Move out. Get a job. Go to college. Move out. Get a job. Go to college.   Move out. Get a job. Go to college. Move out. Get a job. Go to college. Move out. Get a job. Move out. Get a job. Go to college.   Move out. Get a job. Go to college. Move out. Get a job. Go to college.   Move out. Get a job. Go to college. Move out. Get a job. Go to college. Move out. Get a job. Move out. Get a job. Go to college.   Move out. Get a job. Go to college. Move out. Get a job. Go to college.   Move out. Get a job. Go to college. Move out. Get a job. Go to college. Move out. Get a job. Go to college.   Move out. Get a job. Go to college. Move out. Get a job. Go to college. Move out. Get a job. Go to college.   Move out. Get a job. Go to college. Move out. Get a job. Move out. Get a job. Go to college.   Move out. Get a job. Go to college. Move out. Get a job. Go to college.   Move out. Get a job. Go to college. Move out. Get a job. Go to college. Move out. Get a job. Go to college.   Move out. Get a job. Go to college. Move out. Get a job. Go to college. Move out. Get a job. Move out. Get a job. Go to college.   Move out. Get a job. Go

to college. Move out. Get a job. Go to college. Move out.
Get a job. Go to college.   Move out. Get a job. Go to
college. Move out. Get a job. Go to college. Move out.
Get a job. Move out. Get a job. Go to college.   Move
out. Get a job. Go to college. Move out. Get a job. Go
to college. Move out. Get a job. Go to college.   Move
out. Get a job. Go to college. Move out. Get a job. Go
to college. Move out. Get a job. Move out. Get a job. Go
to college.   Move out. Get a job. Go to college. Move
out. Get a job. Go to college. Move out. Get a job. Go
to college.   Move out. Get a job. Go to college. Move
out. Get a job. Go to college. Move out. Get a job. Move
out. Get a job. Go to college.   Move out. Get a job. Go
to college. Move out. Get a job. Go to college. Move out.
Get a job. Go to college.   Move out. Get a job. Go to
college. Move out. Get a job. Go to college. Move out.
Get a job. Move out. Get a job. Go to college.   Move
out. Get a job. Go to college. Move out. Get a job. Go
to college. Move out. Get a job. Go to college.   Move
out. Get a job. Go to college. Move out. Get a job. Go
to college. Move out. Get a job. Move out. Get a job. Go
to college.   Move out. Get a job. Go to college. Move
out. Get a job. Go to college. Move out. Get a job. Go
to college.   Move out. Get a job. Go to college. Move
out. Get a job. Go to college. Move out. Get a job. Move
out. Get a job. Go to college.   Move out. Get a job. Go
to college. Move out. Get a job. Go to college. Move out.
Get a job. Go to college.   Move out. Get a job. Go to
college. Move out. Get a job. Go to college. Move out.
Get a job. Move out. Get a job. Go to college.   Move
out. Get a job. Go to college. Move out. Get a job. Go
to college. Move out. Get a job. Go to college.   Move
out. Get a job. Go to college. Move out. Get a job. Go
to college. Move out. Get a job.

Move out. Get a job. Go to college.   Move out. Get a
job. Go to college. Move out. Get a job. Go to college.
Move out. Get a job. Go to college.   Move out. Get a
job. Go to college. Move out. Get a job. Go to college.

Move out. Get a job. Move out. Get a job. Go to college. Move out. Get a job. Go to college. Move out. Get a job. Go to college. Move out. Get a job. Go to college. Move out. Get a job. Go to college. Move out. Get a job. Go to college. Move out. Get a job. Move out. Get a job. Go to college. Move out. Get a job. Go to college. Move out. Get a job. Go to college. Move out. Get a job. Go to college. Move out. Get a job. Go to college. Move out. Get a job. Move out. Get a job. Go to college. Move out. Get a job. Go to college. Move out. Get a job. Go to college. Move out. Get a job. Go to college. Move out. Get a job.

Move out. Get a job. Go to college. Move out. Get a job. Go to college. Move out. Get a job. Go to college. Move out. Get a job. Go to college. Move out. Get a job. Go to college. Move out. Get a job. Go to college. Move out. Get a job. Move out. Get a job. Go to college. Move out. Get a job. Go to college. Move out. Get a job. Go to college. Move out. Get a job. Go to college. Move out. Get a job. Move out. Get a job. Go to college. Move out. Get a job. Go to college. Move out. Get a job. Go to college. Move out. Get a job. Go to college. Move out. Get a job. Go to college. Move out. Get a job. Move out. Get a job. Go to college. Move out. Get a job. Go to college. Move out. Get a job. Go to college. Move out. Get a job. Go to college. Move out. Get a job. Move out. Get a job. Go to college. Move out. Get a job. Go to college. Move out. Get a job. Go to college. Move out. Get a job. Go to college. Move out. Get a job.

Move out. Get a job. Go to college. Move out. Get a job. Go to college. Move out. Get a job. Go to college.

Move out. Get a job. Go to college. Move out. Get a job. Go to college. Move out. Get a job. Go to college. Move out. Get a job.

Move out. Get a job. Go to college. Move out. Get a job. Go to college. Move out. Get a job. Go to college. Move out. Get a job. Go to college. Move out. Get a job. Go to college. Move out. Get a job.

Move out. Get a job. Go to college. Move out. Get a job. Go to college. Move out. Get a job. Go to college. Move out. Get a job. Go to college. Move out. Get a job. Move out. Get a job. Go to college. Move out. Get a job. Go to college. Move out. Get a job. Go to college. Move out. Get a job. Go to college. Move out. Get a job. Go to college. Move out. Get a job.

Move out. Get a job. Go to college. Move out. Get a job. Go to college. Move out. Get a job. Go to college. Move out. Get a job. Go to college. Move out. Get a job. Move out. Get a job. Go to college. Move out. Get a job. Go to college. Move out. Get a job. Go to college. Move out. Get a job. Go to college. Move out. Get a job.

Move out. Get a job. Go to college. Move out. Get a job. Go to college. Move out. Get a job. Go to college. Move out. Get a job. Go to college. Move out. Get a job.

Move out. Get a job. Go to college. Move out. Get a job. Go to college. Move out. Get a job. Go to college. Move out. Get a job. Go to college. Move out. Get a job.

Move out. Get a job. Go to college.   Move out. Get a job. Go to college. Move out. Get a job. Go to college. Move out. Get a job. Go to college.   Move out. Get a job. Go to college. Move out. Get a job. Go to college. Move out. Get a job.

Move out. Get a job. Go to college.   Move out. Get a job. Go to college. Move out. Get a job. Go to college. Move out. Get a job. Go to college.   Move out. Get a job. Go to college. Move out. Get a job. Go to college. Move out. Get a job. Move out. Get a job. Go to college.   Move out. Get a job. Go to college. Move out. Get a job. Go to college. Move out. Get a job. Go to college.   Move out. Get a job. Go to college. Move out. Get a job. Go to college. Move out. Get a job. Move out. Get a job. Go to college.   Move out. Get a job. Go to college. Move out. Get a job. Go to college. Move out. Get a job. Go to college.   Move out. Get a job. Go to college. Move out. Get a job. Go to college. Move out. Get a job. Move out. Get a job. Go to college.   Move out. Get a job. Go to college. Move out. Get a job. Go to college. Move out. Get a job. Go to college.   Move out. Get a job. Go to college. Move out. Get a job. Go to college. Move out. Get a job. Move out. Get a job. Go to college.   Move out. Get a job. Go to college. Move out. Get a job. Go to college. Move out. Get a job. Go to college.   Move out. Get a job. Go to college. Move out. Get a job. Go to college. Move out. Get a job. Move out. Get a job. Go to college.   Move out. Get a job. Go to college. Move out. Get a job. Go to college. Move out. Get a job. Go to college.   Move out. Get a job. Go to college. Move out. Get a job. Go to college.   Move out. Get a job. Go to college. Move out. Get a job. Go to college. Move out. Get a job. Move out. Get a job. Go to college.   Move out. Get a job. Go to college. Move out. Get a job. Go to college. Move out. Get a job. Go to college.   Move out. Get a job. Go to college. Move out. Get a job. Go to college. Move out. Get a job. Move out. Get a job. Go to college.   Move out. Get a job. Go to college. Move out. Get a job. Go to college. Move out. Get a job. Go to college.   Move out. Get a job. Go to college. Move out. Get a job. Go to college. Move out. Get a job. Move out. Get a job. Go to college.   Move out. Get a job. Go to college. Move out. Get a job. Go to college. Move out. Get a job. Go to college.   Move out. Get a job. Go to college. Move out. Get a job. Go to college. Move out. Get a job. Go to college. Move out. Get a job. Move out. Get a job. Go to college.   Move out. Get a job. Go to college. Move out. Get a job. Go to college. Move out. Get a job. Go to college.   Move out. Get a job. Go to college. Move out. Get a job. Go to college. Move out. Get a job. Move out. Get a job. Go to college.   Move out. Get a job. Go to college. Move out. Get a job. Go to college. Move out. Get a job. Go to college.   Move out. Get a job. Go to college. Move out. Get a job. Go to college. Move out. Get a job. Move out. Get a job. Go to college.   Move out. Get a job. Go to college. Move out. Get a job. Go to college. Move out. Get a job. Go to college.   Move out. Get a job. Go to college. Move out. Get a job. Go to college. Move out. Get a job. Move out. Get a job. Go to college.   Move out. Get a job. Go to college. Move out. Get a job. Go to college.   Move out. Get a job. Go to college. Move out. Get a job.

Move out. Get a job. Go to college.   Move out. Get a job. Go to college. Move out. Get a job. Go to college. Move out. Get a job. Go to college.   Move out. Get a job. Go to college. Move out. Get a job. Go to college. Move out. Get a job. Move out. Get a job. Go to college.   Move out. Get a job. Go to college. Move out. Get a job. Go to college. Move out. Get a job. Go to college.   Move out. Get a job. Go to college. Move out. Get a job. Go to college. Move out. Get a job. Move out. Get a job. Go to college.   Move out. Get a job. Go to college. Move out. Get a job. Go to college. Move out. Get a job. Go to college.   Move out. Get a job. Go to college. Move out. Get a job. Go to college. Move out. Get a job. Move out. Get a job. Go to college.   Move out. Get a job. Go to college. Move out. Get a job. Go to college.   Move out. Get a job. Go to college. Move out. Get a job. Go to college. Move out. Get a job.

Move out. Get a job. Go to college.   Move out. Get a job. Go to college. Move out. Get a job. Go to college. Move out. Get a job. Go to college.   Move out. Get a job. Go to college. Move out. Get a job. Go to college. Move out. Get a job. Move out. Get a job. Go to college. Move out. Get a job. Go to college. Move out. Get a job. Go to college. Move out. Get a job. Go to college. Move out. Get a job. Go to college. Move out. Get a job. Go to college. Move out. Get a job. Go to college.   Move out. Get a job. Go to college. Move out. Get a job. Go to college. Move out. Get a job. Go to college.   Move out. Get a job. Go to college. Move out. Get a job. Go to college. Move out. Get a job. Go to college.   Move out. Get a job. Go to college. Move out. Get a job. Go to college.   Move out. Get a job. Go to college. Move out. Get a job. Go to college. Move out. Get a job. Go to college.   Move out. Get a job. Go to college. Move out. Get a job. Go to college.   Move out. Get a job. Go to college. Move out. Get a job. Go to college. Move out. Get a job.

Move out. Get a job. Go to college.   Move out. Get a job. Go to college. Move out. Get a job. Go to college. Move out. Get a job. Go to college.   Move out. Get a job. Go to college. Move out. Get a job. Go to college. Move out. Get a job.

Move out. Get a job. Go to college.   Move out. Get a job. Go to college. Move out. Get a job. Go to college. Move out. Get a job. Go to college.   Move out. Get a job. Go to college. Move out. Get a job. Go to college. Move out. Get a job.

Move out. Get a job. Go to college.   Move out. Get a job. Go to college. Move out. Get a job. Go to college. Move out. Get a job. Go to college.   Move out. Get a job. Go to college. Move out. Get a job. Go to college. Move out. Get a job. Move out. Get a job. Go to college.   Move out. Get a job. Go to college. Move out. Get a job. Go to college.   Move out. Get a job. Go to college. Move out. Get a job. Go to college. Move out. Get a job.

Move out. Get a job. Go to college.   Move out. Get a job. Go to college. Move out. Get a job. Go to college. Move out. Get a job. Go to college.   Move out. Get a job. Go to college. Move out. Get a job. Go to college. Move out. Get a job. Move out. Get a job. Go to college.   Move out. Get a job. Go to college. Move out. Get a job. Go to college.   Move out. Get a job. Go to college. Move out. Get a job. Go to college. Move out. Get a job.

Move out. Get a job. Go to college.   Move out. Get a job. Go to college. Move out. Get a job. Go to college. Move out. Get a job. Go to college.   Move out. Get a job. Go to college. Move out. Get a job. Go to college. Move out. Get a job.

Move out. Get a job. Go to college. Move out. Get a job. Go to college. Move out. Get a job. Go to college. Move out. Get a job. Go to college. Move out. Get a job. Go to college. Move out. Get a job. Go to college. Move out. Get a job.

Move out. Get a job. Go to college. Move out. Get a job. Go to college. Move out. Get a job. Go to college. Move out. Get a job. Go to college. Move out. Get a job. Go to college. Move out. Get a job. Go to college. Move out. Get a job.

Move out. Get a job. Go to college. Move out. Get a job. Go to college. Move out. Get a job. Go to college. Move out. Get a job. Go to college. Move out. Get a job. Go to college. Move out. Get a job. Go to college. Move out. Get a job. Move out. Get a job. Go to college. Move out. Get a job. Go to college. Move out. Get a job. Go to college. Move out. Get a job. Go to college. Move out. Get a job. Go to college. Move out. Get a job. Go to college. Move out. Get a job. Move out. Get a job. Go to college. Move out. Get a job. Go to college. Move out. Get a job. Go to college. Move out. Get a job. Go to college. Move out. Get a job. Go to college. Move out. Get a job. Go to college. Move out. Get a job. Move out. Get a job. Go to college. Move out. Get a job. Go to college. Move out. Get a job. Go to college. Move out. Get a job. Go to college. Move out. Get a job. Go to college. Move out. Get a job. Go to college. Move out. Get a job. Move out. Get a job. Go to college. Move out. Get a job. Go to college. Move out. Get a job. Go to college. Move out. Get a job. Go to college. Move out. Get a job. Go to college. Move out. Get a job. Go to college. Move out. Get a job. Move out. Get a job. Go to college. Move out. Get a job. Go to college. Move out. Get a job. Go to college. Move out. Get a job. Go to college. Move out. Get a job. Go to college. Move out. Get a job. Go to college. Move out. Get a job. Move out. Get a job. Go to college. Move out. Get a job. Go to college. Move out. Get a job. Go to college. Move out. Get a job. Go to college. Move out. Get a job. Go to college. Move out. Get a job. Go to college. Move out. Get a job. Move out. Get a job. Go to college. Move out. Get a job. Go to college. Move out. Get a job. Go to college. Move out. Get a job. Go to college. Move out. Get a job. Go to college. Move out. Get a job. Move out. Get a job. Go to college. Move out. Get a job. Go to college. Move out. Get a job. Go to college. Move out. Get a job. Go to Get a job. Go to college. Move out. Get a job. Go to college. Move out. Get a job. Go to college. Move out. Get a job. Move out. Get a job. Go to college. Move out. Get a job. Go to college. Move out. Get a job. Go to college. Move out. Get a job. Go to college. Move out. Get a job. Go to college. Move out. Get a job. Move out. Get a job. Go to college. Move out. Get a job. Go to college. Move out. Get a job. Go to college. Move out. Get a job. Go to college. Move out. Get a job. Go to college. Move out. Get a job. Move out. Get a job. Go to college. Move out. Get a job. Go to college. Move out. Get a job. Go to Get a job. Go to college. Move out. Get a job. Go to college. Move out. Get a job. Go to college. Move out. Get a job. Move out. Get a job. Go to college. Move out. Get a job. Go to college. Move out. Get a job. Go to college. Move out. Get a job. Go to college. Move out. Get a job. Go to college. Move out. Get a job. Move out. Get a job. Go to college. Move out. Get a job. Go to college. Move out. Get a job. Go to college. Move out. Get a job. Go to college. Move out. Get a job. Go to college. Move out. Get a job. Go to Get a job. Go to college. Move out. Get a job. Go to college. Move out. Get a job. Go to college. Move out. Get a job. Move out. Get a job. Go to college. Move

80

out. Get a job. Go to college. Move out. Get a job. Go to college. Move out. Get a job. Go to college.   Move out. Get a job. Go to college. Move out. Get a job. Go to college. Move out. Get a job.

Move out. Get a job. Go to college.   Move out. Get a job. Go to college. Move out. Get a job. Go to college. Move out. Get a job. Go to college.   Move out. Get a job. Go to college. Move out. Get a job. Go to college. Move out. Get a job. Move out. Get a job. Go to college.   Move out. Get a job. Go to college. Move out. Get a job. Go to college. Move out. Get a job. Go to college.   Move out. Get a job. Go to college. Move out. Get a job. Go to college. Move out. Get a job. Move out. Get a job. Go to college.   Move out. Get a job. Go to college. Move out. Get a job. Go to college. Move out. Get a job. Go to college.   Move out. Get a job. Go to college. Move out. Get a job. Go to college. Move out. Get a job. Move out. Get a job. Go to college.   Move out. Get a job. Go to college. Move out. Get a job. Go to college.   Move out. Get a job. Go to college. Move out. Get a job. Go to college. Move out. Get a job.

Move out. Get a job. Go to college.   Move out. Get a job. Go to college. Move out. Get a job. Go to college. Move out. Get a job. Go to college.   Move out. Get a job. Go to college. Move out. Get a job. Go to college. Move out. Get a job. Move out. Get a job. Go to college. Move out. Get a job. Go to college. Move out. Get a job. Go to college. Move out. Get a job. Go to college.   Move out. Get a job. Go to college. Move out. Get a job. Go to college. Move out. Get a job. Move out. Get a job. Go to college.   Move out. Get a job. Go to college. Move out. Get a job. Go to college. Move out. Get a job. Go to college.   Move out. Get a job. Go to college. Move out. Get a job. Go to college. Move out. Get a job. Move out. Get a job. Go to college.   Move out. Get a job. Go to college. Move out. Get a job. Go to college.   Move

out. Get a job. Go to college. Move out. Get a job. Go to college. Move out. Get a job. Move out. Get a job. Go to college.   Move out. Get a job. Go to college. Move out. Get a job. Go to college. Move out. Get a job. Go to college.   Move out. Get a job. Go to college. Move out. Get a job. Go to college. Move out. Get a job.

Move out. Get a job. Go to college.   Move out. Get a job. Go to college. Move out. Get a job. Go to college. Move out. Get a job. Go to college.   Move out. Get a job. Go to college. Move out. Get a job. Go to college. Move out. Get a job.

Move out. Get a job. Go to college.   Move out. Get a job. Go to college. Move out. Get a job. Go to college. Move out. Get a job. Go to college.   Move out. Get a job. Go to college. Move out. Get a job. Go to college. Move out. Get a job.

Move out. Get a job. Go to college.   Move out. Get a job. Go to college. Move out. Get a job. Go to college. Move out. Get a job. Go to college.   Move out. Get a job. Go to college. Move out. Get a job. Go to college. Move out. Get a job. Move out. Get a job. Go to college.   Move out. Get a job. Go to college. Move out. Get a job. Go to college. Move out. Get a job. Go to college.   Move out. Get a job. Go to college. Move out. Get a job. Go to college. Move out. Get a job.

Move out. Get a job. Go to college.   Move out. Get a job. Go to college. Move out. Get a job. Go to college. Move out. Get a job. Go to college.   Move out. Get a job. Go to college. Move out. Get a job. Go to college. Move out. Get a job. Move out. Get a job. Go to college.   Move out. Get a job. Go to college. Move out. Get a job. Go to college. Move out. Get a job. Go to college.   Move out. Get a job. Go to college. Move out. Get a job. Go to college. Move out. Get a job.

Move out. Get a job. Go to college.   Move out. Get a job. Go to college. Move out. Get a job. Go to college.

Move out. Get a job. Go to college.   Move out. Get a job. Go to college. Move out. Get a job. Go to college. Move out. Get a job.

Move out. Get a job. Go to college.   Move out. Get a job. Go to college. Move out. Get a job. Go to college. Move out. Get a job. Go to college.   Move out. Get a job. Go to college. Move out. Get a job. Go to college. Move out. Get a job.

Move out. Get a job. Go to college.   Move out. Get a job. Go to college. Move out. Get a job. Go to college. Move out. Get a job. Go to college.   Move out. Get a job. Go to college. Move out. Get a job. Go to college. Move out. Get a job.

Move out. Get a job. Go to college.   Move out. Get a job. Go to college. Move out. Get a job. Go to college. Move out. Get a job. Go to college.   Move out. Get a job. Go to college. Move out. Get a job. Go to college. Move out. Get a job. Move out. Get a job. Go to college.   Move out. Get a job. Go to college. Move out. Get a job. Go to college.   Move out. Get a job. Go to college. Move out. Get a job. Go to college. Move out. Get a job. Move out. Get a job. Go to college.   Move out. Get a job. Go to college. Move out. Get a job. Go to college.   Move out. Get a job. Go to college. Move out. Get a job. Go to college. Move out. Get a job. Move out. Get a job. Go to college.   Move out. Get a job. Go to college. Move out. Get a job. Go to college. Move out. Get a job. Go to college.   Move out. Get a job. Go to college. Move out. Get a job. Go to college. Move out. Get a job. Move out. Get a job. Go to college.   Move out. Get a job. Go to college. Move out. Get a job. Go to college.   Move out. Get a job. Go to college. Move out. Get a job. Go to college.   Move out. Get a job. Go to college. Move out.

Get a job. Go to college. Move out. Get a job. Go to college. Move out. Get a job. Go to college. Move out. Get a job. Move out. Get a job. Go to college. Move out. Get a job. Go to college. Move out. Get a job. Go to college. Move out. Get a job. Go to college. Move out. Get a job. Go to college. Move out. Get a job. Go to college. Move out. Get a job. Move out. Get a job. Go to college. Move out. Get a job. Go to college. Move out. Get a job. Go to college. Move out. Get a job. Go to college. Move out. Get a job. Go to college. Move out. Get a job. Go to college. Move out. Get a job. Go to college. Move out. Get a job. Go to college. Move out. Get a job. Go to college. Move out. Get a job. Go to college. Move out. Get a job. Go to college. Move out. Get a job. Go to college. Move out. Get a job. Go to college. Move out. Get a job. Move out. Get a job. Go to college. Move out. Get a job. Go to college. Move out. Get a job. Go to college. Move out. Get a job. Go to college. Move out. Get a job. Go to college. Move out. Get a job. Go to college. Move out. Get a job. Go to college. Move out. Get a job. Go to college. Move out. Get a job. Go to college. Move out. Get a job. Go to college. Move out. Get a job. Go to college. Move out. Get a job. Go to college. Move out. Get a job. Move out. Get a job. Go to college. Move out. Get a job. Go to college. Move out. Get a job. Go to college. Move out. Get a job. Go to college. Move out. Get a job. Go to college. Move out. Get a job. Go to college. Move out. Get a job. Go to college. Move out. Get a job. Go to college. Move out. Get a job. Go to college. Move out. Get a job. Go to college. Move out. Get a job. Go to college. Move out. Get a job. Go to college. Move out. Get a job. Move out. Get a job. Go to college. Move out. Get a job. Go to college. Move out. Get a job. Go to college. Move out. Get a job. Go to college.   Move out. Get a job. Go to college. Move out. Get a job. Go to college. Move out. Get a job. Move out. Get a job. Go to college.   Move out. Get a job. Go to college. Move out. Get a job. Go to college. Move out. Get a job. Go to college.   Move out. Get a job. Go to college. Move out. Get a job. Go to college. Move out. Get a job.

Move out. Get a job. Go to college.   Move out. Get a job. Go to college. Move out. Get a job. Go to college. Move out. Get a job. Go to college.   Move out. Get a job. Go to college. Move out. Get a job. Go to college. Move out. Get a job. Move out. Get a job. Go to college.   Move out. Get a job. Go to college. Move out. Get a job. Go to college. Move out. Get a job. Go to college.   Move out. Get a job. Go to college. Move out. Get a job. Go to college. Move out. Get a job. Go to college.   Move out. Get a job. Go to college. Move out. Get a job. Go to college. Move out. Get a job. Go to college.   Move out. Get a job. Go to college. Move out. Get a job. Go to college. Move out. Get a job. Go to college.   Move out. Get a job. Go to college. Move out. Get a job. Go to college.   Move out. Get a job. Go to college. Move out. Get a job. Go to college.   Move out. Get a job. Go to college. Move out. Get a job.

Move out. Get a job. Go to college.   Move out. Get a job. Go to college. Move out. Get a job. Go to college. Move out. Get a job. Go to college.   Move out. Get a job. Go to college. Move out. Get a job. Go to college. Move out. Get a job. Move out. Get a job. Go to college. Move out. Get a job. Go to college. Move out. Get a job. Go to college. Move out. Get a job. Go to college. Move out. Get a job. Go to college. Move out. Get a job. Go to college. Move out. Get a job.   Move out. Get a job. Go to college. Move out. Get a job. Go to college.   Move out. Get a job. Go to college. Move out. Get a job. Go to college. Move out. Get a job. Move out. Get a job. Go to college.   Move out. Get a job. Go to college. Move out. Get a job. Go to college. Move out. Get a job. Go to college.   Move out. Get a job. Go to college. Move out. Get a job. Go to college. Move out. Get a job. Move out. Get a job. Go to college.   Move out. Get a job. Go to college. Move out. Get a job. Go to college. Move out. Get a job. Go to college. Move out. Get a job. Go to college. Move out. Get a job.

Move out. Get a job. Go to college.   Move out. Get a job. Go to college. Move out. Get a job. Go to college. Move out. Get a job. Go to college.   Move out. Get a job. Go to college. Move out. Get a job. Go to college. Move out. Get a job.

Move out. Get a job. Go to college.   Move out. Get a job. Go to college. Move out. Get a job. Go to college. Move out. Get a job. Go to college.   Move out. Get a job. Go to college. Move out. Get a job. Go to college. Move out. Get a job.

Move out. Get a job. Go to college.   Move out. Get a job. Go to college. Move out. Get a job. Go to college. Move out. Get a job. Go to college.   Move out. Get a job. Go to college. Move out. Get a job. Go to college. Move out. Get a job. Move out. Get a job. Go to college.   Move out. Get a job. Go to college. Move out. Get a job. Go to college.   Move out. Get a job. Go to college. Move out. Get a job. Go to college. Move out. Get a job.

Move out. Get a job. Go to college.   Move out. Get a job. Go to college. Move out. Get a job. Go to college.   Move out. Get a job. Go to college. Move out. Get a job. Go to college. Move out. Get a job. Move out. Get a job. Go to college.   Move out. Get a job. Go to college. Move out. Get a job. Go to college. Move out. Get a job. Go to college. Move out. Get a job. Go to college. Move out. Get a job. Go to college. Move out. Get a job.

Move out. Get a job. Go to college. Move out. Get a job. Go to college. Move out. Get a job. Go to college. Move out. Get a job. Go to college. Move out. Get a job. Go to college. Move out. Get a job. Go to college. Move out. Get a job.

Move out. Get a job. Go to college. Move out. Get a job. Go to college. Move out. Get a job. Go to college. Move out. Get a job. Go to college. Move out. Get a job. Go to college. Move out. Get a job. Go to college. Move out. Get a job.

Move out. Get a job. Go to college. Move out. Get a job. Go to college. Move out. Get a job. Go to college. Move out. Get a job. Go to college. Move out. Get a job. Go to college. Move out. Get a job. Go to college. Move out. Get a job.

Move out. Get a job. Go to college. Move out. Get a job. Go to college. Move out. Get a job. Go to college. Move out. Get a job. Go to college. Move out. Get a job. Go to college. Move out. Get a job. Go to college. Move out. Get a job. Move out. Get a job. Go to college. Move out. Get a job. Go to college. Move out. Get a job. Go to college. Move out. Get a job. Go to college. Move out. Get a job. Go to college. Move out. Get a job. Move out. Get a job. Go to college. Move out. Get a job. Go to college. Move out. Get a job. Go to college. Move out. Get a job. Go to college. Move out. Get a job. Go to college. Move out. Get a job. Go to college. Move out. Get a job. Move out. Get a job. Go to college. Move out. Get a job. Go to college. Move out. Get a job. Go to college. Move out. Get a job. Go to college. Move out. Get a job. Move out. Get a job. Go to college. Move out. Get a job. Go to college. Move out. Get a job. Go to college. Move up to college.   Move out. Get a job. Go to college. Move out. Get a job. Go to college. Move out. Get a job. Move out. Get a job. Go to college.   Move out. Get a job. Go to college. Move out. Get a job. Go to college. Move out. Get a job. Go to college.   Move out. Get a job. Go to college. Move out. Get a job. Go to college. Move out. Get a job. Move out. Get a job. Go to college.   Move out. Get a job. Go to college. Move out. Get a job. Go to college. Move out. Get a job. Go to college.   Move out. Get a job. Go to college. Move out. Get a job. Go to college. Move out. Get a job. Go to college.   Move out. Get a job. Go to college. Move out. Get a job. Go to college. Move out. Get a job. Move out. Get a job. Go to college.   Move out. Get a job. Go to college. Move out. Get a job. Go to college. Move out. Get a job. Go to college.   Move out. Get a job. Go to college. Move out. Get a job. Go to college. Move out. Get a job. Move out. Get a job. Go to college.   Move out. Get a job. Go to college. Move out. Get a job. Go to college. Move out. Get a job. Go to college.   Move out. Get a job. Go to college. Move out. Get a job. Go to college. Move out. Get a job. Go to college.   Move out. Get a job. Go to college. Move out. Get a job. Go to college. Move out. Get a job. Go to college.   Move out. Get a job. Go to college. Move out. Get a job. Go to college. Move out. Get a job. Move out. Get a job. Go to college.   Move out. Get a job. Go to college. Move out. Get a job. Go to college. Move out. Get a job. Go to college.   Move out. Get a job. Go to college. Move out. Get a job. Go to college. Move out. Get a job. Go to college.   Move out. Get a job. Go to college. Move out. Get a job. Go to college. Move out. Get a job. Go to college. Move out. Get a job. Move out. Get a job. Go to college.   Move out. Get a job. Go to college. Move out. Get a job. Go to college. Move out. Get a job. Go to college.   Move out. Get a job. Go to college. Move out. Get a job. Go to college. Move out. Get a job. Move out. Get a job. Go to college.   Move out. Get a job. Go to college. Move out. Get a job. Go to college. Move out. Get a job. Go to college.   Move out. Get a job. Go to college. Move out. Get a job. Go to college. Move out. Get a job. Move out. Get a job. Go to college.   Move out. Get a job. Go to college. Move out. Get a job. Go to college. Move out. Get a job. Go to college.   Move out. Get a job. Go to college. Move out. Get a job. Go to college. Move out. Get a job. Go to college. Move out. Get a job.

Move out. Get a job. Go to college.   Move out. Get a job. Go to college. Move out. Get a job. Go to college. Move out. Get a job. Go to college.   Move out. Get a job. Go to college. Move out. Get a job. Go to college. Move out. Get a job. Move out. Get a job. Go to college.   Move out. Get a job. Go to college. Move out. Get a job. Go to college. Move out. Get a job. Go to college. Move out. Get a job. Go to college. Move out. Get a job. Move out. Get a job. Go to college.   Move out. Get a job. Go to college. Move out. Get a job. Go to college. Move out. Get a job. Go to college.   Move out. Get a job. Go to college. Move out. Get a job. Move out. Get a job. Go to college.   Move out. Get a job. Go to college. Move out. Get a job. Go to college.   Move out. Get a job. Go to college. Move out. Get a job. Go to college. Move out. Get a job.

Move out. Get a job. Go to college.   Move out. Get a job. Go to college. Move out. Get a job. Go to college. Move out. Get a job. Go to college.   Move out. Get a job. Go to college. Move out. Get a job. Go to college. Move out. Get a job. Move out. Get a job. Go to college. Move out. Get a job. Go to college. Move out. Get a job. Go to college. Move out. Get a job. Go to college. Move out. Get a job. Go to college. Move out.

89

Get a job. Go to college. Move out. Get a job. Move out. Get a job. Go to college. Move out. Get a job. Go to college. Move out. Get a job. Go to college. Move out. Get a job. Go to college. Move out. Get a job. Go to college. Move out. Get a job. Go to college. Move out. Get a job. Move out. Get a job. Go to college. Move out. Get a job. Go to college. Move out. Get a job. Go to college. Move out. Get a job. Go to college. Move out. Get a job. Go to college. Move out. Get a job. Go to college. Move out. Get a job. Move out. Get a job. Go to college. Move out. Get a job. Go to college. Move out. Get a job. Go to college. Move out. Get a job. Go to college. Move out. Get a job. Go to college. Move out. Get a job.

Move out. Get a job. Go to college. Move out. Get a job. Go to college. Move out. Get a job. Go to college. Move out. Get a job. Go to college. Move out. Get a job. Go to college. Move out. Get a job. Go to college. Move out. Get a job.

Move out. Get a job. Go to college. Move out. Get a job. Go to college. Move out. Get a job. Go to college. Move out. Get a job. Go to college. Move out. Get a job. Go to college. Move out. Get a job. Go to college. Move out. Get a job.

Move out. Get a job. Go to college. Move out. Get a job. Go to college. Move out. Get a job. Go to college. Move out. Get a job. Go to college. Move out. Get a job. Go to college. Move out. Get a job. Go to college. Move out. Get a job. Move out. Get a job. Go to college. Move out. Get a job. Go to college. Move out. Get a job. Go to college. Move out. Get a job. Go to college. Move out. Get a job. Go to college. Move out. Get a job.

Move out. Get a job. Go to college. Move out. Get a job. Go to college. Move out. Get a job. Go to college. Move out. Get a job. Go to college. Move out. Get a job. Go to college. Move out. Get a job. Go to college.

Move out. Get a job. Move out. Get a job. Go to college. Move out. Get a job. Go to college. Move out. Get a job. Go to college. Move out. Get a job. Go to college. Move out. Get a job. Go to college. Move out. Get a job. Go to college. Move out. Get a job.

Move out. Get a job. Go to college. Move out. Get a job. Go to college. Move out. Get a job. Go to college. Move out. Get a job. Go to college. Move out. Get a job. Go to college. Move out. Get a job. Go to college. Move out. Get a job.

Move out. Get a job. Go to college. Move out. Get a job. Go to college. Move out. Get a job. Go to college. Move out. Get a job. Go to college. Move out. Get a job. Go to college. Move out. Get a job. Go to college. Move out. Get a job.

Move out. Get a job. Go to college. Move out. Get a job. Go to college. Move out. Get a job. Go to college. Move out. Get a job. Go to college. Move out. Get a job. Go to college. Move out. Get a job. Go to college. Move out. Get a job.

Move out. Get a job. Go to college. Move out. Get a job. Go to college. Move out. Get a job. Go to college. Move out. Get a job. Go to college. Move out. Get a job. Go to college. Move out. Get a job. Go to college. Move out. Get a job. Move out. Get a job. Go to college. Move out. Get a job. Go to college. Move out. Get a job. Go to college. Move out. Get a job. Go to college. Move out. Get a job. Go to college. Move out. Get a job. Move out. Get a job. Go to college. Move out. Get a job. Go to college. Move out. Get a job. Go to college. Move out. Get a job. Go to college. Move out. Get a job. Go to college. Move out. Get a job. Go to college. Move out. Get a job. Move out. Get a job. Go to college. Move out. Get a job. Go to college. Move out. Get a job. Go to college. Move out. Get a job. Go to college. Move out. Get a job. Go to college. Move out. Get a job. Go to college. Move out. Get a job. Go to college. Move out. Get a job. Move out. Get a job. Go to college. Move out. Get a job. Go to college. Move out. Get a job. Go to college. Move out. Get a job. Go to college. Move out. Get a job. Go to college. Move out. Get a job. Go to college. Move out. Get a job. Move out. Get a job. Go to college. Move out. Get a job. Go to college. Move out. Get a job. Go to college. Move out. Get a job. Go to college. Move out. Get a job. Go to college. Get a job. Go to college. Move out. Get a job. Go to college. Move out. Get a job. Go to college. Move out. Get a job. Move out. Get a job. Go to college. Move out. Get a job. Go to college. Move out. Get a job. Go to college. Move out. Get a job. Go to college. Move out. Get a job. Go to college. Move out. Get a job. Go to college. Move out. Get a job. Go to college. Move out. Get a job. Go to college. Move out. Get a job. Move out. Get a job. Go to college. Move out. Get a job. Go to college. Move out. Get a job. Go to college. Move out. Get a job. Go to college. Move out. Get a job. Go to college. Get a job. Go to college. Move out. Get a job. Go to college. Move out. Get a job. Go to college. Move out. Get a job. Move out. Get a job. Go to college. Move out. Get a job. Go to college. Move out. Get a job. Go to college. Move out. Get a job. Go to college. Move out. Get a job. Go to college. Move out. Get a job. Go to college. Move out. Get a job. Go to college. Move out. Get a job. Go to college. Move out. Get a job. Move out. Get a job. Go to college. Move out. Get a job. Go to college. Move out. Get a job. Go to college. Move out. Get a job. Go to college. Move out. Get a job. Go to college. Get a job. Go to college. Move out. Get a job. Go to college. Move out. Get a job. Go to college. Move out. Get a job. Move out. Get a job. Go to college. Move out. Get a job. Go to college. Move out. Get a job. Go to college. Move out. Get a job. Go to college. Move out. Get a job. Go to college. Move out. Get a job. Move out. Get a job. Go to college. Move out. Get a job. Go to college. Move out. Get a job. Go to college. Move out. Get a job. Go to college. Move out. Get a job. Go to college. Move out. Get a job. Go to college. Move out. Get a job. Move out. Get a job. Go to college. Move out. Get a job. Go to college. Move out. Get a job. Go to college. Move out. Get a job. Go to college. Move out. Get a job. Go to college. Move out. Get a job. Go to college. Move out. Get a job. Move out. Get a job. Go to college. Move out. Get a job. Go to college. Move out. Get a job. Go to college. Move out. Get a job. Go to college. Move out. Get a job. Go to college. Move out. Get a job. Go to college. Move out. Get a job.

Move out. Get a job. Go to college. Move out. Get a job. Go to college. Move out. Get a job. Go to college. Move out. Get a job. Go to college. Move out. Get a job. Go to college. Move out. Get a job. Go to college. Move out. Get a job. Move out. Get a job. Go to college. Move out. Get a job. Go to college. Move out. Get a job. Go to college. Move out. Get a job. Go to college. Move out. Get a job. Go to college. Move out. Get a job. Go to college. Move out. Get a job. Move out. Get a job. Go to college. Move out. Get a job. Go to college. Move out. Get a job. Go to college. Move out. Get a job. Go to college. Move out. Get a job. Go to college. Move out. Get a job. Go to college. Move out. Get a job. Move out. Get a job. Go to college. Move out. Get a job. Go to college. Move out. Get a job. Go to college. Move out. Get a job. Go to college. Move out. Get a job. Go to college. Move out. Get a job. Go to college. Move out. Get a job.

Move out. Get a job. Go to college. Move out. Get a job. Go to college. Move out. Get a job. Go to college. Move out. Get a job. Go to college. Move out. Get a job. Go to college. Move out. Get a job. Go to college. Move out. Get a job. Move out. Get a job. Go to

college. Move out. Get a job. Go to college. Move out. Get a job. Go to college. Move out. Get a job. Go to college. Move out. Get a job. Go to college. Move out. Get a job. Go to college. Move out. Get a job. Move out. Get a job. Go to college. Move out. Get a job. Go to college. Move out. Get a job. Go to college. Move out. Get a job. Go to college. Move out. Get a job. Go to college. Move out. Get a job. Move out. Get a job. Go to college. Move out. Get a job. Go to college. Move out. Get a job. Go to college. Move out. Get a job. Go to college. Move out. Get a job. Move out. Get a job. Go to college. Move out. Get a job. Go to college. Move out. Get a job. Go to college. Move out. Get a job. Go to college. Move out. Get a job. Go to college. Move out. Get a job.

Move out. Get a job. Go to college. Move out. Get a job. Go to college. Move out. Get a job. Go to college. Move out. Get a job. Go to college. Move out. Get a job. Go to college. Move out. Get a job. Go to college. Move out. Get a job.

Move out. Get a job. Go to college. Move out. Get a job. Go to college. Move out. Get a job. Go to college. Move out. Get a job. Go to college. Move out. Get a job. Go to college. Move out. Get a job. Go to college. Move out. Get a job.

Move out. Get a job. Go to college. Move out. Get a job. Go to college. Move out. Get a job. Go to college. Move out. Get a job. Go to college. Move out. Get a job. Go to college. Move out. Get a job. Go to college. Move out. Get a job. Move out. Get a job. Go to college. Move out. Get a job. Go to college. Move out. Get a job. Go to college. Move out. Get a job. Go to college. Move out. Get a job. Go to college. Move out. Get a job.

Move out. Get a job. Go to college.   Move out. Get a
job. Go to college. Move out. Get a job. Go to college.
Move out. Get a job. Go to college.   Move out. Get a
job. Go to college. Move out. Get a job. Go to college.
Move out. Get a job. Move out. Get a job. Go to
college.   Move out. Get a job. Go to college. Move out.
Get a job. Go to college. Move out. Get a job. Go to
college.   Move out. Get a job. Go to college. Move out.
Get a job. Go to college. Move out. Get a job.

Move out. Get a job. Go to college.   Move out. Get a
job. Go to college. Move out. Get a job. Go to college.
Move out. Get a job. Go to college.   Move out. Get a
job. Go to college. Move out. Get a job. Go to college.
Move out. Get a job.

Move out. Get a job. Go to college.   Move out. Get a
job. Go to college. Move out. Get a job. Go to college.
Move out. Get a job. Go to college.   Move out. Get a
job. Go to college. Move out. Get a job. Go to college.
Move out. Get a job.

Move out. Get a job. Go to college.   Move out. Get a
job. Go to college. Move out. Get a job. Go to college.
Move out. Get a job. Go to college.   Move out. Get a
job. Go to college. Move out. Get a job. Go to college.
Move out. Get a job.

Move out. Get a job. Go to college.   Move out. Get a
job. Go to college. Move out. Get a job. Go to college.
Move out. Get a job. Go to college.   Move out. Get a
job. Go to college. Move out. Get a job. Go to college.
Move out. Get a job. Move out. Get a job. Go to
college.   Move out. Get a job. Go to college. Move out.
Get a job. Go to college. Move out. Get a job. Go to
college.   Move out. Get a job. Go to college. Move out.
Get a job. Go to college. Move out. Get a job. Move out.
Get a job. Go to college.   Move out. Get a job. Go to
college. Move out. Get a job. Go to college. Move out.
Get a job. Go to college.   Move out. Get a job. Go to
college. Move out. Get a job. Go to college. Move out.

Get a job. Move out. Get a job. Go to college. Move out. Get a job. Go to college. Move out. Get a job. Go to college. Move out. Get a job. Go to college. Move out. Get a job. Go to college. Move out. Get a job. Go to college. Move out. Get a job. Move out. Get a job. Go to college. Move out. Get a job. Go to college. Move out. Get a job. Go to college. Move out. Get a job. Go to college. Move out. Get a job. Go to college. Move out. Get a job. Move out. Get a job. Go to college. Move out. Get a job. Go to college. Move out. Get a job. Go to college. Move out. Get a job. Go to college. Move out. Get a job. Go to college. Move out. Get a job. Go to college. Move out. Get a job. Move out. Get a job. Go to college. Move out. Get a job. Go to college. Move out. Get a job. Go to college. Move out. Get a job. Go to college. Move out. Get a job. Go to college. Move out. Get a job. Go to college. Move out. Get a job. Move out. Get a job. Go to college. Move out. Get a job. Go to college. Move out. Get a job. Go to college. Move out. Get a job. Go to college. Move out. Get a job. Go to college. Move out. Get a job. Go to college. Move out. Get a job. Move out. Get a job. Go to college. Move out. Get a job. Go to college. Move out. Get a job. Go to college. Move out. Get a job. Move out. Get a job. Go to college. Move out. Get a job. Go to college. Move out. Get a job. Go to college. Move out. Get a job. Go to college. Move out. Get a job. Go to college. Move out. Get a job. Move out. Get a job. Go to college.   Move out. Get a job. Go to college. Move out. Get a job. Go to college. Move out. Get a job. Go to college.   Move out. Get a job. Go to college. Move out. Get a job. Go to college. Move out. Get a job. Move out. Get a job. Go to college.   Move out. Get a job. Go to college. Move out. Get a job. Go to college.   Move out. Get a job. Go to college. Move out. Get a job. Move out. Get a job. Go to college.   Move out. Get a job. Go to college. Move out. Get a job. Go to college. Move out. Get a job. Go to college.   Move out. Get a job. Go to college. Move out. Get a job. Move out. Get a job. Go to college.   Move out. Get a job. Go to college. Move out. Get a job. Go to college. Move out. Get a job. Go to college.   Move out. Get a job. Go to college. Move out. Get a job. Go to college. Move out. Get a job.

Move out. Get a job. Go to college.   Move out. Get a job. Go to college. Move out. Get a job. Go to college. Move out. Get a job. Go to college.   Move out. Get a job. Go to college. Move out. Get a job. Go to college. Move out. Get a job. Move out. Get a job. Go to college.   Move out. Get a job. Go to college. Move out. Get a job. Go to college. Move out. Get a job. Go to college.   Move out. Get a job. Go to college. Move out. Get a job. Go to college. Move out. Get a job. Move out. Get a job. Go to college.   Move out. Get a job. Go to college. Move out. Get a job. Go to college. Move out. Get a job. Go to college.   Move out. Get a job. Go to college. Move out. Get a job. Go to college. Move out. Get a job. Move out. Get a job. Go to college.   Move out. Get a job. Go to college. Move out. Get a job. Go to college.   Move out. Get a job. Go to college. Move out. Get a job. Go to college. Move out. Get a job.

Move out. Get a job. Go to college.   Move out. Get a job. Go to college. Move out. Get a job. Go to college. Move out. Get a job. Go to college.   Move out. Get a job. Go to college. Move out. Get a job. Go to college. Move out. Get a job. Move out. Get a job. Go to college. Move out. Get a job. Go to college. Move out. Get a job. Go to college. Move out. Get a job. Go to college. Move out. Get a job. Go to college. Move out. Get a job. Move out. Get a job. Go to college.   Move out. Get a job. Go to college. Move out. Get a job. Go to college. Move out. Get a job. Go to college.   Move out. Get a job. Go to college. Move out. Get a job. Move out. Get a job. Go to college.   Move out. Get a job. Go to college. Move out. Get a job. Go to college.   Move out. Get a job. Go to college. Move out. Get a job. Go to college. Move out. Get a job. Move out. Get a job. Go to college.   Move out. Get a job. Go to college. Move out. Get a job. Go to college.   Move out. Get a job. Go to college. Move out. Get a job. Go to college. Move out. Get a job. Go to college. Move out. Get a job.

Move out. Get a job. Go to college.   Move out. Get a job. Go to college. Move out. Get a job. Go to college. Move out. Get a job. Go to college.   Move out. Get a job. Go to college. Move out. Get a job. Go to college. Move out. Get a job.

Move out. Get a job. Go to college.   Move out. Get a job. Go to college. Move out. Get a job. Go to college. Move out. Get a job. Go to college.   Move out. Get a job. Go to college. Move out. Get a job. Go to college. Move out. Get a job.

Move out. Get a job. Go to college.   Move out. Get a job. Go to college. Move out. Get a job. Go to college. Move out. Get a job. Go to college.   Move out. Get a job. Go to college. Move out. Get a job. Go to college. Move out. Get a job. Move out. Get a job. Go to

college.   Move out. Get a job. Go to college. Move out. Get a job. Go to college. Move out. Get a job. Go to college.   Move out. Get a job. Go to college. Move out. Get a job. Go to college. Move out. Get a job.

Move out. Get a job. Go to college.   Move out. Get a job. Go to college. Move out. Get a job. Go to college. Move out. Get a job. Go to college.   Move out. Get a job. Go to college. Move out. Get a job. Go to college. Move out. Get a job. Move out. Get a job. Go to college.   Move out. Get a job. Go to college. Move out. Get a job. Go to college. Move out. Get a job. Go to college.   Move out. Get a job. Go to college. Move out. Get a job. Go to college. Move out. Get a job.

Move out. Get a job. Go to college.   Move out. Get a job. Go to college. Move out. Get a job. Go to college. Move out. Get a job. Go to college.   Move out. Get a job. Go to college. Move out. Get a job. Go to college. Move out. Get a job.

Move out. Get a job. Go to college.   Move out. Get a job. Go to college. Move out. Get a job. Go to college. Move out. Get a job. Go to college.   Move out. Get a job. Go to college. Move out. Get a job. Go to college. Move out. Get a job.

Move out. Get a job. Go to college.   Move out. Get a job. Go to college. Move out. Get a job. Go to college. Move out. Get a job. Go to college.   Move out. Get a job. Go to college. Move out. Get a job. Go to college. Move out. Get a job.

Move out. Get a job. Go to college.   Move out. Get a job. Go to college. Move out. Get a job. Go to college. Move out. Get a job. Go to college.   Move out. Get a job. Go to college. Move out. Get a job. Move out. Get a job. Go to college.   Move out. Get a job. Go to college. Move out. Get a job. Go to college. Move out. Get a job. Go to college.   Move out. Get a job. Go to college. Move out.

Get a job. Go to college. Move out. Get a job. Move out. Get a job. Go to college. Move out. Get a job. Go to college. Move out. Get a job. Go to college. Move out. Get a job. Go to college. Move out. Get a job. Go to college. Move out. Get a job. Go to college. Move out. Get a job. Move out. Get a job. Go to college. Move out. Get a job. Go to college. Move out. Get a job. Go to college. Move out. Get a job. Go to college. Move out. Get a job. Go to college. Move out. Get a job. Go to college. Move out. Get a job. Go to college. Move out. Get a job. Go to college. Move out. Get a job. Move out. Get a job. Go to college. Move out. Get a job. Go to college. Move out. Get a job. Go to college. Move out. Get a job. Go to college. Move out. Get a job. Go to college. Move out. Get a job. Go to college. Move out. Get a job. Go to college. Move out. Get a job. Go to college. Move out. Get a job. Move out. Get a job. Go to college. Move out. Get a job. Go to college. Move out. Get a job. Go to college. Move out. Get a job. Go to college. Move out. Get a job. Go to college. Move out. Get a job. Go to college. Move out. Get a job. Go to college. Move out. Get a job. Go to college. Move out. Get a job. Move out. Get a job. Go to college. Move out. Get a job. Go to college. Move out. Get a job. Go to college. Move out. Get a job. Go to college. Move out. Get a job. Go to college. Move out. Get a job. Go to college. Move out. Get a job. Go to college. Move out. Get a job. Go

to college.   Move out. Get a job. Go to college. Move
out. Get a job. Go to college. Move out. Get a job. Move
out. Get a job. Go to college.   Move out. Get a job. Go
to college. Move out. Get a job. Go to college. Move out.
Get a job. Go to college.   Move out. Get a job. Go to
college. Move out. Get a job. Go to college. Move out.
Get a job. Move out. Get a job. Go to college.   Move
out. Get a job. Go to college. Move out. Get a job. Go
to college. Move out. Get a job. Go to college.   Move
out. Get a job. Go to college. Move out. Get a job. Go
to college. Move out. Get a job. Move out. Get a job. Go
to college.   Move out. Get a job. Go to college. Move
out. Get a job. Go to college. Move out. Get a job. Go
to college.   Move out. Get a job. Go to college. Move
out. Get a job. Go to college. Move out. Get a job. Move
out. Get a job. Go to college.   Move out. Get a job. Go
to college. Move out. Get a job. Go to college. Move out.
Get a job. Go to college.   Move out. Get a job. Go to
college. Move out. Get a job. Go to college. Move out.
Get a job. Move out. Get a job. Go to college.   Move
out. Get a job. Go to college. Move out. Get a job. Go
to college. Move out. Get a job. Go to college.   Move
out. Get a job. Go to college. Move out. Get a job. Go
to college. Move out. Get a job.

Move out. Get a job. Go to college.   Move out. Get a
job. Go to college. Move out. Get a job. Go to college.
Move out. Get a job. Go to college.   Move out. Get a
job. Go to college. Move out. Get a job. Go to college.
Move out. Get a job. Move out. Get a job. Go to
college.   Move out. Get a job. Go to college. Move out.
Get a job. Go to college. Move out. Get a job. Go to
college.   Move out. Get a job. Go to college. Move out.
Get a job. Go to college. Move out. Get a job. Move out.
Get a job. Go to college.   Move out. Get a job. Go to
college. Move out. Get a job. Go to college. Move out.
Get a job. Go to college.   Move out. Get a job. Go to
college. Move out. Get a job. Go to college. Move out.
Get a job. Move out. Get a job. Go to college.   Move

out. Get a job. Go to college. Move out. Get a job. Go to college. Move out. Get a job. Go to college.   Move out. Get a job. Go to college. Move out. Get a job. Go to college. Move out. Get a job.

Move out. Get a job. Go to college.   Move out. Get a job. Go to college. Move out. Get a job. Go to college. Move out. Get a job. Go to college.   Move out. Get a job. Go to college. Move out. Get a job. Go to college. Move out. Get a job. Move out. Get a job. Go to college. Move out. Get a job. Go to college. Move out. Get a job. Go to college. Move out. Get a job. Go to college. Move out. Get a job. Go to college. Move out. Get a job. Move out. Get a job. Go to college.   Move out. Get a job. Go to college. Move out. Get a job. Go to college. Move out. Get a job. Go to college.   Move out. Get a job. Go to college. Move out. Get a job. Go to college. Move out. Get a job. Move out. Get a job. Go to college.   Move out. Get a job. Go to college. Move out. Get a job. Go to college.   Move out. Get a job. Go to college. Move out. Get a job. Go to college. Move out. Get a job. Move out. Get a job. Go to college.   Move out. Get a job. Go to college. Move out. Get a job. Go to college.   Move out. Get a job. Go to college. Move out. Get a job. Go to college. Move out. Get a job. Go to college. Move out. Get a job.

Move out. Get a job. Go to college.   Move out. Get a job. Go to college. Move out. Get a job. Go to college. Move out. Get a job. Go to college.   Move out. Get a job. Go to college. Move out. Get a job. Go to college. Move out. Get a job.

Move out. Get a job. Go to college.   Move out. Get a job. Go to college. Move out. Get a job. Go to college.   Move out. Get a job. Go to college. Move out. Get a job. Go to college. Move out. Get a job.

Move out. Get a job. Go to college.   Move out. Get a job. Go to college. Move out. Get a job. Go to college. Move out. Get a job. Go to college.   Move out. Get a job. Go to college. Move out. Get a job. Go to college. Move out. Get a job. Move out. Get a job. Go to college.   Move out. Get a job. Go to college. Move out. Get a job. Go to college. Move out. Get a job. Go to college.   Move out. Get a job. Go to college. Move out. Get a job. Go to college. Move out. Get a job.

Move out. Get a job. Go to college.   Move out. Get a job. Go to college. Move out. Get a job. Go to college. Move out. Get a job. Go to college.   Move out. Get a job. Go to college. Move out. Get a job. Go to college. Move out. Get a job. Move out. Get a job. Go to college.   Move out. Get a job. Go to college. Move out. Get a job. Go to college. Move out. Get a job. Go to college.   Move out. Get a job. Go to college. Move out. Get a job. Go to college. Move out. Get a job.

Move out. Get a job. Go to college.   Move out. Get a job. Go to college. Move out. Get a job. Go to college. Move out. Get a job. Go to college.   Move out. Get a job. Go to college. Move out. Get a job. Go to college. Move out. Get a job.

Move out. Get a job. Go to college.   Move out. Get a job. Go to college. Move out. Get a job. Go to college. Move out. Get a job. Go to college.   Move out. Get a job. Go to college. Move out. Get a job. Go to college. Move out. Get a job.

Move out. Get a job. Go to college.   Move out. Get a job. Go to college. Move out. Get a job. Go to college. Move out. Get a job. Go to college.   Move out. Get a job. Go to college. Move out. Get a job. Go to college. Move out. Get a job.

Move out. Get a job. Go to college.   Move out. Get a job. Go to college. Move out. Get a job. Go to college. Move out. Get a job. Go to college.   Move out. Get a job. Go to college. Move out. Get a job. Go to college. Move out. Get a job. Move out. Get a job. Go to college. Move out. Get a job. Go to college. Move out. Get a job. Go to college. Move out. Get a job. Go to college. Move out. Get a job. Go to college. Move out. Get a job. Go to college. Move out. Get a job. Move out. Get a job. Go to college. Move out. Get a job. Go to college. Move out. Get a job. Go to college. Move out. Get a job. Go to college. Move out. Get a job. Go to college. Move out. Get a job. Move out. Get a job. Go to college. Move out. Get a job. Go to college. Move out. Get a job. Go to college. Move out. Get a job. Go to college. Move out. Get a job. Move out. Get a job. Go to college. Move out. Get a job. Go to college. Move out. Get a job. Go to college. Move out. Get a job. Go to college. Move out. Get a job. Go to college. Move out. Get a job. Move out. Get a job. Go to college. Move out. Get a job. Go to college. Move out. Get a job. Go to college. Move out. Get a job. Go to college. Move out. Get a job. Move out. Get a job. Go to college. Move out. Get a job. Go to college. Move out. Get a job. Go to college. Move out. Get a job. Go to college. Move out. Get a job. Go to college. Move out. Get a job. Move out. Get a job. Go to college. Move out. Get a job. Go to college. Move out. Get a job. Go to college. Move out. Get a job. Go to college. Move out. Get a job. Move out. Get a job. Go to college. Move out. Get a job. Go to college. Move out. Get a job. Go to college. Move out. Get a job. Go to college. Move out. Get a job. Go to college. Move out. Get a job. Go to college. Move out. Get a job. Move out. Get a job. Go to college. Move out. Get a job. Go to college. Move out. Get a job. Go to college. Move out. Get a job. Go to college. Move out. Get a job. Go to college. Move out. Get a job. Move out. Get a job. Go to college. Move out. Get a job. Go to college. Move out. Get a job. Go to college. Move out. Get a job. Go to college. Move out. Get a job. Go to college. Move out. Get a job. Go to college. Move out. Get a job. Go to college. Move out. Get a job. Go to college. Move out. Get a job. Move out. Get a job. Go to college. Move out. Get a job. Go to college. Move out. Get a job. Go to college. Move out. Get a job. Go to college. Move out. Get a job. Go to college. Move out. Get a job. Go to college. Move out. Get a job. Move out. Get a job. Go to college. Move out. Get a job. Go to college. Move out. Get a job. Go to college. Move out. Get a job. Go to college. Move out. Get a job. Go to college. Move out. Get a job. Move out. Get a job. Go to college. Move out. Get a job. Go to college. Move out. Get a job. Go to college. Move out. Get a job. Go to college. Move out. Get a job.

Move out. Get a job. Go to college. Move out. Get a job. Go to college. Move out. Get a job. Go to college. Move out. Get a job. Go to college. Move out. Get a job. Go to college. Move out. Get a job. Go to college. Move out. Get a job. Move out. Get a job. Go to college. Move out. Get a job. Go to college. Move out. Get a job. Go to college. Move out. Get a job. Go to college. Move out. Get a job. Go to college. Move out. Get a job. Go to college. Move out.

105

Get a job. Go to college.   Move out. Get a job. Go to college. Move out. Get a job. Go to college. Move out. Get a job. Go to college.   Move out. Get a job. Go to college. Move out. Get a job. Go to college. Move out. Get a job. Move out. Get a job. Go to college.   Move out. Get a job. Go to college. Move out. Get a job. Go to college. Move out. Get a job. Go to college.   Move out. Get a job. Go to college. Move out. Get a job. Go to college. Move out. Get a job.

Move out. Get a job. Go to college.   Move out. Get a job. Go to college. Move out. Get a job. Go to college. Move out. Get a job. Go to college.   Move out. Get a job. Go to college. Move out. Get a job. Go to college. Move out. Get a job. Move out. Get a job. Go to college.   Move out. Get a job. Go to college. Move out. Get a job. Go to college.   Move out. Get a job. Go to college.   Move out. Get a job. Go to college. Move out. Get a job. Move out. Get a job. Go to college. Move out. Get a job. Go to college.   Move out. Get a job. Go to college. Move out. Get a job. Go to college. Move out. Get a job. Go to college.   Move out. Get a job. Go to college. Move out. Get a job. Go to college. Move out. Get a job. Move out. Get a job. Go to college.   Move out. Get a job. Go to college. Move out. Get a job. Go to college.   Move out. Get a job. Go to college. Move out. Get a job. Go to college. Move out. Get a job. Go to college.   Move out. Get a job. Go to college. Move out. Get a job. Go to college.   Move out. Get a job. Go to college. Move out. Get a job. Go to college. Move out. Get a job.

Move out. Get a job. Go to college.   Move out. Get a job. Go to college. Move out. Get a job. Go to college. Move out. Get a job. Go to college.   Move out. Get a job. Go to college. Move out. Get a job. Go to college. Move out. Get a job.

Printed in Great Britain
by Amazon